## 英検®とは？

　文部科学省後援　実用英語技能検定（通称：英検®）は，英語の4技能「読む・聞く・話す・書く」を総合的に測定する試験です。1963年に第1回検定が実施されて以来，日本社会の国際化に伴ってその社会的評価が高まり，現在では，学校・自治体などの団体を対象とした英語力判定テスト「英検IBA®」，子どもを対象としたリスニングテスト「英検Jr.®」を合わせると，年間約420万人が受験しています。大学入試や高校入試，就職試験でも，英語力を測るものさしとして活用されており，入試においての活用校も年々増えています。アメリカ，オーストラリアを中心に，海外でも英検®は，数多くの大学・大学院などの教育機関で，留学時の語学力証明資格として認められています（英検®を語学力証明として認定している海外の教育機関は英検®ウェブサイトに掲載されています）。

## 本書の使い方

　本書は，2021年度第3回から2023年度第2回まで過去6回分の試験問題を掲載した，過去問題集です。**6回分すべてのリスニング問題CDがついています**ので，過去6回の本試験と同じ練習を行うことができます。また，リスニング問題の小問ごとにトラック番号を設定していますので，自分の弱点を知ること，そしてその弱点を強化するためにくり返し問題を聞くことができます。

　また本書では，**出題されやすい「文法事項」と「イディオム・口語表現」**を，効率的に学習できるよう分類ごとにまとめてあります。過去問題と併せて活用していただければ幸いです。

　英検®では，能力を公正に測定するという試験の性格上，各回・各年度ほぼ同レベルの問題が出されます。したがって，試験の傾向はある程度限定されたパターンをとることになりますので，過去の試験問題をくり返し解き，本試験へと備えてください。

　本書を利用される皆様が，一日も早く栄冠を勝ちとられますよう，心より祈念いたします。

　英検®，英検Jr.®，英検IBA®は，公益財団法人　日本英語検定協会の登録商標です。

# 2022年度

●**第3回検定**

一次試験・筆記 ················································· 98

**CD** 一次試験・リスニング（**CD赤-1〜26**）············· 114

二次試験・面接 ············································· 120

第3回　解答・解説 ········································· 別冊 91

●**第2回検定**

一次試験・筆記 ················································· 126

**CD** 一次試験・リスニング（**CD赤-27〜52**）·········· 142

二次試験・面接 ············································· 148

第2回　解答・解説 ········································· 別冊 135

●**第1回検定**

一次試験・筆記 ················································· 154

**CD** 一次試験・リスニング（**CD緑-1〜26**）············· 170

二次試験・面接 ············································· 176

第1回　解答・解説 ········································· 別冊 179

# 2021年度

●**第3回検定**

一次試験・筆記 ················································· 182

**CD** 一次試験・リスニング（**CD緑-27〜52**）·········· 198

二次試験・面接 ············································· 204

第3回　解答・解説 ········································· 別冊 223

本書は，原則として 2024 年 1 月 15 日現在の情報に基づいて編集しています。

# 受験ガイド

## 2024年度　試験日程（本会場）

二次試験は2日間設定されています。

| | | | | |
|---|---|---|---|---|
| 第1回 | 申込期間 | 2024年3月15日〜5月5日（書店は4月19日締切） | | |
| | 試験日程 | 一次試験 | 2024年6月2日（日） | |
| | | 二次試験 | A日程 | 2024年7月7日（日） |
| | | | B日程 | 2024年7月14日（日） |
| 第2回 | 申込期間 | 2024年7月1日〜9月6日（書店は8月30日締切） | | |
| | 試験日程 | 一次試験 | 2024年10月6日（日） | |
| | | 二次試験 | A日程 | 2024年11月10日（日） |
| | | | B日程 | 2024年11月17日（日） |
| 第3回 | 申込期間 | 2024年11月1日〜12月13日（書店は12月6日締切） | | |
| | 試験日程 | 一次試験 | 2025年1月26日（日） | |
| | | 二次試験 | A日程 | 2025年3月2日（日） |
| | | | B日程 | 2025年3月9日（日） |

※二次試験日程は年齢によって決まります。詳しくは英検®ウェブサイトでご確認ください。
※クレジットカード決済の場合，申込締切は上記の日付の3日後になります。

## 申込方法

① 個人申込
　・特約書店・・・検定料を払い込み，「書店払込証書」と「願書」を必着日までに
　　　協会へ郵送。
　・インターネット・・・英検®ウェブサイト（https://www.eiken.or.jp/
　　　eiken/）から申込。
　・コンビニ申込・・・ローソン・ミニストップ「Loppi」，セブン-イレブン・ファ
　　　ミリーマート「マルチコピー機」などの情報端末機から
　　　申し込み。
　問い合わせ先　公益財団法人 日本英語検定協会
　　　　　　　　TEL 03-3266-8311　英検®サービスセンター（個人受付）
　　　　　　　　（平日9:30〜17:00　土・日・祝日を除く）
② 団体申込
　団体申込に関しましては各団体の責任者の指示に従ってお申し込みください。

## 成績表

成績表には合否結果のほかに，英検バンド，英検CSEスコアも表示されます。

●**英検バンド**　一次試験，二次試験の合格スコアを起点として，自分がいる位置を＋，－で示したものです。例えば，英検バンドの値が＋1ならばぎりぎりで合格，－1ならば，もう少しのところで合格だったということがわかります。

●**英検CSEスコア**　欧米で広く導入されている，語学能力のレベルを示すCEFR（Common European Framework of Reference for Languages）に関連づけて作られた，リーディング，リスニング，ライティング，スピーキングの4技能を評価する尺度です。英検®のテスト結果の，4技能それぞれのレベルと総合のレベルがスコアとして出されます。

## 一次試験免除等

一次試験に合格し，二次試験を棄権または不合格になった人に対して，一次試験免除制度があります。申込時に申請をすれば，一次試験合格から1年間は一次試験が免除されます。検定料は，一次試験を受ける場合と同様にかかります。

※検定料，試験時間については英検®ウェブサイトでご確認ください。

## 英検S-CBTについて

　実用英語技能検定準1級，2級，準2級，3級で，新方式英検S-CBTが毎月実施されています。従来型の英検®，英検S-CBTのどちらの方式でも，合格すれば同じ資格が得られます。英検S-CBTの合格証書・証明書とも，従来型の英検®と全く同じものとなります。

### ◎英検S-CBTの試験実施方法
- コンピューターで4技能（リーディング，ライティング，リスニング，スピーキング）すべてを1日で受験することになります。
- 通常の英検®と同じ検定試験で，問題構成・レベルも通常の英検®と同じです。
- 英検S-CBTはスピーキングテスト（通常の英検®の二次試験），リスニングテスト，リーディングテスト，ライティングテストの順に試験が行われます。
- リーディングテスト，ライティングテスト，リスニングテストのCSEスコアに基づいて一次試験の合否が判定されますが，一次試験の合否にかかわらず，すべての受験者が4技能を受験し，4技能のCSEスコアを取得することになります。一次試験合格者のみスピーキングテストのCSEスコアに基づき二次試験の合否が判定されます。
- 試験はパソコン上で行われるため，Windowsパソコンの基本的な操作（マウスクリック，キーボード入力）ができる必要があります。ただし，ライティングテストはキーボード入力か筆記のいずれかの解答方法を申込時に選択します。

※従来型の試験で二次試験不合格の場合，一次試験免除申請をして英検S-CBTでスピーキングテストのみを受験することができます。

※英検S-CBTで一次試験に合格，二次試験不合格となった場合は，一次試験免除資格が与えられます。次回以降に，一次試験免除申請をして，従来型の英検®を申し込むことができます。

## 英検S-CBT受験ガイド

### ◎試験実施月
※原則として毎週土曜日・日曜日，一部会場においては平日・祝日も実施されます。詳しくは英検®ウェブサイトをご参照ください。

　第1回…4月，5月，6月，7月
　第2回…8月，9月，10月，11月
　第3回…12月，翌年1月，2月，3月

## ◎持参するもの
●英検S-CBT受験票，身分証明書。身分証明書として認められるのは，学生証・生徒手帳・健康保険証・運転免許証・パスポート・社員証・住民基本台帳カード・マイナンバーカード・在留カード・健康保険証のコピー（年少者のみ）です。

## ◎申し込み
●申し込みは先着順です。個人申込のみで団体申込は受け付けていません。
●申し込み時に指定した会場で受験します。会場ごとに定員があり，定員になり次第締め切られます。
●英検S-CBT受験票は申込サイトからダウンロードします。

※検定料，試験時間については英検®ウェブサイトでご確認ください。

## ——————— 英検S-CBTスピーキングテストについて ———————
●英検S-CBTのスピーキングテストとは，通常の英検®の二次試験で行われる面接試験のことです。
●英検S-CBTではコンピューターの映像を通して面接委員とやり取りし，録音形式で試験が行われます。
●試験の内容やレベルは通常の英検®二次試験と同じです。二次試験の試験内容については11，19ページをご参照ください。
●英検S-CBTの，特にスピーキングテストではヘッドセットやマイクの使い方，音量の調整にある程度慣れておく必要があります。

　英検S-CBTはパソコン上で行われるため，試験当日の流れ，受験方法の面で通常の英検®と異なるところもあります。特に，最初にスピーキングテストが行われる点は大きな違いです。通常の英検®の二次試験と同じと言っても，面接委員と直接対面するか，画面を通して対面するかという違い，パソコンの操作があるかないかという違いは決して小さなことではありません。試験当日の流れ，受験方法の面で通常の英検®と異なるところについては，受験前に必ず英検®ウェブサイトでしっかり確認して，落ち着いてスピーキングテストに臨めるようにしましょう。

# 準1級受験の注意点

## 解答用紙の記入についての注意

筆記試験，リスニングテストともに，別紙の解答用紙にマークシート方式で解答します。解答にあたっては，次の点に留意してください。

**1** 解答用紙には，はじめに氏名，生年月日などを記入します。生年月日はマーク欄をぬりつぶす指示もありますので，忘れずにマークしてください。

　不正確な記入は答案が無効になることもあるので注意してください。

**2** マークはHBの黒鉛筆またはシャープペンシルを使って「マーク例」に示された以上の濃さで正確にぬりつぶします。

　解答の訂正は，プラスチックの消しゴムで完全に消してから行ってください。

**3** 解答用紙を汚したり折り曲げたりすることは厳禁です。また，所定の欄以外は絶対に記入しないでください。

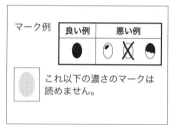

## 準1級のめやすと試験の形式

### ●準1級のめやす

準1級のレベルは大学中級程度で，社会生活で求められる英語を理解し，使用できることが求められます。

〈審査領域〉

**読む**……社会性の高い分野の文章を理解することができる。

**聞く**……社会性の高い内容を理解することができる。

**話す**……社会性の高い話題についてやりとりすることができる。

**書く**……社会性の高い話題についてまとまりのある文章を書くことができる。

### ●準1級試験の内容と形式

一次試験ではまずはじめに筆記試験が行われ，その後にリスニングテストが行われます。二次試験は英語での面接試験で，一次試験の合格者のみを対象とし，一次試験実施後およそ30日後に行われます。

## 一次試験・筆記（33問・90分）

　筆記試験は，4つの大問で構成されており，問題数は33問です（2024年度第1回検定から）。この33問の問題を90分かけて解きます。

2024年度第1回の検定から，問題構成・内容は以下の通りです。

| 大問 | 内容 | 問題数 |
|---|---|---|
| 1 | **短文または会話文の穴うめ問題**<br>短文または1往復の会話文を読み，文中の空所に適切な語句を補う。 | 18問 |
| 2 | **長文の穴うめ問題**<br>説明文，評論文などを読み，パッセージの空所に，文脈に合う適切な語句を補う。 | 6問 |
| 3 | **長文の内容に関する問題**<br>説明文，評論文などを読み，これらの英文の内容に関する質問に答える。 | 7問 |
| 4 | **英語の文章の要約を英語で記述する問題**<br>200語程度の文章の要約を60〜70語程度で書く。<br>**与えられたトピックに対し，意見とその根拠を英文で論述する問題**<br>あるトピックに関する質問に対して，自分の意見とその理由を書く。 | 2問<br>（記述式） |

## 一次試験・リスニング（29問・約30分）

　リスニングテストは，第1部〜第3部で構成されており，問題数は29問です。この29問の問題を約30分かけて解きます。

| 大問 | 内容 | 問題数 |
|---|---|---|
| 1 | **会話の内容に関する質問**<br>会話文を聞き，会話の内容に関する質問に答える。 | 12問 |
| 2 | **英文の内容に関する質問**<br>説明文を聞き，その内容に関する質問に答える。 | 12問 |
| 3 | **Real-Life形式の放送内容に関する質問**<br>自分自身が置かれている状況や場面を読んだうえでアナウンスなどを聞き，その内容に関する質問に答える。 | 5問 |

《一次試験で用いられた主な場面と題材》
　場面………家庭，学校，職場，地域（各種店舗・公共施設を含む），電話，アナウンス，講義など。
　題材………社会生活一般，芸術，文化，歴史，教育，科学，自然・環境，医療，テクノロジー，ビジネス，政治など。

## 二次試験・面接（約8分）

　二次試験は，約8分の受験者対面接委員の1対1の面接です。**面接室への入室から退室までのすべてが採点の対象になり，応答内容，発音，語い，文法，語法，情報量，積極的にコミュニケーションを図ろうとする意欲や態度**などで評価されます。

## ●二次試験の流れ

① 面接室に入室します。面接委員にあいさつをするとよいでしょう（Good morning./Good afternoon.）。

② 着席するよう指示されます。着席後，名前と受験する級の確認などを含めて簡単な質問をされるほか，面接委員と日常的な会話を行います。

③ 英語で指示が書かれた4コマのイラストつきカードが1枚渡されます。カードを黙読し，イラスト内容のナレーションを考える時間が1分与えられます。

④ その後，カードの指示文に従ってナレーションを始めるよう指示が出されます。ナレーションの言い出し部分は「問題カード」に印刷されていますから，必ずその言い出し部分を使って，ナレーションを始めます。ナレーションの時間は2分間です。それ以上続く場合は，途中でも中止させられます。

⑤ その後，4つの質問が出題されます。最初の質問の後でカードを伏せるよう指示（Please turn over the card. など）が出たら，すみやかに伏せてください。
　●質問1‥‥‥イラストに関連した質問。
　●質問2，3‥‥カードのトピックに関連した質問。
　●質問4‥‥‥カードのトピックにやや関連した，社会性のある内容についての質問。質問の前に，話題を導入する文が示されます（2024年度第1回の検定より）。

---

**《二次試験で用いられた主な話題》**
在宅勤務，レストランでの喫煙，チャイルドシート，住民運動，キャッチセールス，護身術など。

---

# 準1級の傾向と対策

　英検®は出題パターンがある程度決まっています。2024年度第1回の検定から
ライティングテストの形式と筆記試験の問題数が一部変更されますが, 全体とし
て大きな違いはありませんので, 過去の問題を何度も解いて傾向をつかみましょう。
慣れてきたら, 本番を想定した時間配分で解いてみると効果的です。

## 一次試験・筆記テスト

## 1 短文または会話文の穴うめ問題

### ★出題傾向

　短文または会話文の (　　) の中に適する単語または語句を4つの選択肢から
選び, 英文を完成させる。単語→イディオムの出題順がほぼ定着している。
※2024年度第1回の検定から, 問題数が25問から18問になりました。

### 対策

- 単語とイディオムの知識が問われる。
- 単語で出題されるのは, 名詞, 動詞, 形容詞などの基本的な品詞がほとん
  どである。
- イディオムでは句動詞（break into, stand byなど）が中心。

## 2 長文の穴うめ問題

### ★出題傾向

・説明文, 評論文の空所にあてはまるものを, 複数の語句からなる選択肢から
　選ぶ。大問が2題あり, それぞれに空所が3箇所ずつある。選択肢はそれぞ
　れ4つ。

### ●長文の体裁

　3段落構成の説明文, 評論文。語数は250語～300語程度。

### ●長文のテーマ

　過去2年間で出題されたテーマは, 最近の題材を中心として, 自然科学, 環境,
社会情勢・問題, 医療に関するものがほとんどである。

- （　　）前後の文脈を正確に把握し，論理的展開と矛盾しない答えを選ぶ能力が要求される。
- （　　）の前後にある語句との文法的なつながり，時制には特に注意が必要。
- 2大問中，1〜2問は空所に適する接続語句を選ぶ問題なので，空所前後の関係を読み取る能力に加え，接続語句の知識が必要。
- イディオムや決まった形の表現の知識も必要である。

# 3 長文の内容に関する問題

## ★出題傾向

　説明文，評論文の内容についての質問に対する解答を選ぶものと，内容を表す文を完成させるのに適する英語を選ぶものがある。大問が2題あり，最初の大問は小問3題，2つめの大問は小問4題。選択肢はそれぞれ4つである。
※2024年度第1回の検定から，大問数が3題から2題になりました。

## ●長文の体裁

　3〜5段落構成の説明文，評論文。2024年度第1回の検定からは，400語程度と520語程度の2題になることが予想される。

## ●長文のテーマ

　最近の題材を中心として，自然科学，科学技術，環境，社会情勢・問題，文化，法律，医療，教育などをテーマとした英文が出題されている。

### 対 策

- タイトルと第1段落冒頭から，その英文で論じられている主題をつかむ。
- 設問は，段落の順番つまり論旨展開の流れにそって用意されるのがふつうである。これを逆に利用し，「質問文→対応する段落」の順番で読んでいけば，短時間で段落ごとの論点を見つけることができる。
- 各段落や英文全体の論点をつかむうえで重要なポイントとなるのは，①代名詞や代動詞表現（do, do it, do thisなど），②接続語句，③同じ内容の言い換え，④対照表現など。
- 選択肢の英文は本文そのままではなく，同じ意味の語句で言い換えられたり，簡潔に表現されたりしていることが多い。

# 4 ライティングテスト

## ★出題傾向
※2024年度第1回の検定から，文章の要約を書く問題が追加されました。

### ●要約問題
　200語程度の文章の内容を60〜70語程度の英語で要約する。その際，できる限り自分の言葉で書くという条件がある。

### ●意見論述問題
　与えられたトピックについて120語〜150語でエッセイを書く。その際，①与えられているPOINTSから2つを選んで自分の考えを支持する内容（理由，例など）を盛り込む，②「導入→本文→結論」という構成にする，という条件がある。

　質問文では，Should A 〜「Aは〜するべきか」，Agree or disagree「賛成か，反対か」などで始まる英文の中で具体的なトピックが示される。

　自分の考えを支持する英文の観点となるPOINTSが4つ示される。

### ●テーマ
　要約問題，意見論述問題ともに，注目度の高い，社会的な問題に関するトピックが予測される。

## 対策

- 主語，動詞の一致などの基本的なことを含め，文法的に正しい英文を書く。
- 理由を述べる文では，becauseなど，「理由」であることをはっきりさせる語句を使う。
- 語数の過不足に注意する。
- 意見論述問題では，質問内容を正しくつかむ。
- 意見論述問題では，与えられているPOINTSから必ず2つを選ぶ。

## ★ライティングテストの採点に関する観点と注意点
　ライティングテストの採点にあたっての観点と解答作成時の注意点は以下のとおりである。

### ●採点の観点
#### 1．内容
**要約問題：与えられた英文の内容が正しく書かれているか**

　要約文を書くので，与えられた英文の内容と異なることを書いたり，自分の考えや感情などを盛り込まないようにする。

**意見論述問題：課題で求められている内容（意見とその理由）が含まれているかどうか**

　自分の意見とその理由をはっきりさせ，意見を支える論拠や説明を説得力のあるものにする。単に「安いから」や「便利だから」といったことだけではなく，安くなったり便利になったりすることで生じる具体的な利点を挙げる。

**２．構成**

**要約問題：与えられた英文の構成に沿っているか**

　与えられた英文の段落構成と同じ構成,流れでまとめる。英文が「テーマの提示」→「テーマとなるもののプラス面」→「テーマとなるもののマイナス面」という流れであれば，それと同じ流れで要約文を構成する。

**意見論述問題：英文の構成や流れがわかりやすく論理的であるか**

　伝える情報を羅列するのではなく，順番や流れを論理的にする。展開を示す接続語句を正しく使って，自分の意見とその理由，英文全体の構成をわかりやすくする。

**３．語い　課題に相応しい語いを正しく使えているか**

　なるべく多様な語いや表現を使い，同じ語いや表現の繰り返しを避ける。

**４．文法　文構造のバリエーションやそれらを正しく使えているか**

　多様な文のパターンを使い，同じような構文の繰り返しを避ける。


**●意見論述問題解答作成時の注意点**

　英検®ウェブサイトでは，「カジュアルな服装を許容する会社が増えるかどうか」というTOPICを例に挙げて,解答作成にあたっての下記の注意点が公開されている。それぞれの詳細と具体例をウェブサイトで確認しておこう。

**１．TOPICに示された問いに答えていない**

　TOPICに示された問いの答えになっていない場合や，全く関係のないTOPICについて書かれていると判断された場合は，上記のすべての観点で0点と採点されることがある。

**２．英語ではない単語を使った解答**

　英語以外の単語を使う必要がある場合は，その言語を理解できない人にもわかるように説明を加える。そうした説明がない場合は減点の対象となる。

**３．意見と矛盾する理由や説明がある**

　自分が述べた意見に矛盾する内容の理由や説明を書いてある。

**４．理由に対する説明や補足がない**

　理由について，具体的な例や説明がなく，説得力に欠ける。

**5. 関係のない内容が含まれている**

TOPICに示された問いに無関係の内容や，他の部分と矛盾する内容が書かれている。

## 一次試験・リスニングテスト

### 対策（全リスニング問題共通）

英文はすべて1回しか読まれない。全体で約30分，合計29題のリスニングでは，集中力をいかに持続させるかも聞き取りの重要なポイントとなる。また，指示文はすべて英語で読まれるので，あらかじめ試験形式を把握しておくことが必要。

## 【第1部】会話の内容に関する質問

### ★出題傾向

70語〜100語程度の会話（電話での会話も含む）を聞き，その内容に関する質問の答えを4つの選択肢から選ぶ。

### ●放送されるもの

会話→質問文。

- 放送文が始まる前に，問題用紙の選択肢に目を通しておき，会話の場面や質問の内容（場所，状況，時間，人物の行動など）を予想する。
- 会話の内容はさまざまで，家庭や職場などでの代表的なシチュエーションが次々と登場する。放送文ごとに素早く頭を切り換えることが大切。
- 放送文の一部が聞き取れなくても，全体として状況がつかめれば，消去法で選択肢を絞り込み，正解に到達できることが多い。
- 会話文中に現れる質問文，命令文，依頼文などには特に注意。
- 会話文中に難しい固有名詞が現れることもあるが，聞き取れなくても，少なくともそれが人名なのか地名なのかという段階で理解することが大切。

## 【第2部】文の内容に関する質問

### ★出題傾向

2段落から成る130語～150語の文章を聞き，その内容に関する質問の答えを4つの選択肢から選ぶ。1つの文章につき，質問が2つあり，1つの段落について1問ずつ用意されている。

### ●放送されるもの

英文→質問文。

対 策

- 第1部同様，放送文が始まる前に選択肢に目を通しておくと，聞き取りのポイントを絞ることができる。
- 英文の種類は，基本的に毎回すべて説明文である。テーマは自然科学，科学技術，環境，社会情勢・問題，文化，医療など。
- 説明文なので，第1文からテーマがわかることが多い。
- 逆接のbutやhoweverが出てきた直後の内容や，因果関係を述べている箇所は，特に注意して聞き取るようにする。質問で尋ねてくる確率が高い。
- 難しい固有名詞が出てくることが多いので，正確に聞き取れなくても，それが人名なのか地名なのかという段階で理解できるようにする。
- 西暦や数量を表す数字は質問に絡んでくる場合が多い。

# 【第３部】 Real-Life形式の放送内容に関する質問

## ★出題傾向

自分自身が置かれている状況を読んだうえでアナウンスなどを聞き，その内容に関する質問の答えを４つの選択肢から選ぶ。

## ●読むもの・放送されるもの

読むもの：問題用紙に，自分が置かれている状況を示すSituationと質問，答えの選択肢４つが書かれている。Situationは家庭，職場，旅行先，店など，実生活に則した場面でのさまざまな状況。放送の前に，Situationと質問を読む時間が10秒与えられる。

放送されるもの：それぞれのSituationでのアナウンス，店員の発言，家族・友人・同僚などからの電話など。

### 対策

- Situationの内容をよく読んで，自分が置かれている状況を理解する。未経験の状況である場合もあるので，想像力を働かせる必要もある。
- 選択肢は，名詞句，不定詞で始まるもの，動詞の原形で始まるものなど，それぞれの問題で同じ形になっている場合がほとんどなので，Situationと質問から放送される内容と聞き取りのポイントを予想する。
- 質問はwhatまたはwhichで始まるものがほとんどで，自分がとるべき行動を問うものなので，自分がするべきことを予想することで聞き取りのポイントもつかみやすくなる。
- 解答者自身がするべきことを問われるので，放送文中からわかる周囲の状況のほかに，指示や依頼を述べている箇所には特に注意が必要。

# 二次試験・面接

**★出題傾向**

　問題カードには英文の指示と４コマのイラストが印刷されている。面接試験は，以下のような流れで行われる。

　①面接委員と簡単な日常会話を行う

　②英文を黙読し，イラスト内容を説明するナレーションを考える（１分間）

　③カードの指示文に従ってナレーションを行う（２分間）

　④イラストの４コマ目に関する質問（No. 1）

　⑤カードのトピックに関連する質問（No. 2，3）

　⑥カードのトピックにやや関連した，社会性のある内容に関する質問（No. 4）

　※2024年度第１回の検定から，No. 4の質問の前に話題が示されます。

## 対策

- 答えの正確さ（発音・語い・文法など）のほか，情報量や表現方法（意欲や態度を含む）も評価対象となる。入退室時の挨拶，ナレーションの前の面接委員との会話も含めて，十分な声量で自信を持って受け答えしよう。

- 面接委員が尋ねる質問は，問題カードに書かれていないので，その質問内容を正確に聞き取ることが重要となる。

- ナレーションに続く４つの質問は，いずれも解答者の意見を問うもので，イラストの内容を正しく理解し，質問に対して短時間で答えを出す必要がある。質問は社会全般に関わるものなので，日頃から社会で起こっている事柄や社会情勢に関心を持ち，自分の基本的な考えをまとめておくことが重要。できるだけ面接委員と視線を合わせながら答える姿勢も大切。

- No. 1ではイラスト４コマ目を見て，もし自分がイラストの人物だったらどう考えるかを問われる。最初の黙読の段階で自分の基本的な意見を決めておき，答えるときはそのように考える理由も加えるべきである。

- No. 2と3は原則として，カードのトピックに関する意見や考え方に同意するかしないかを問う質問だが，ここでも根拠となることや具体例などを加え，意見としてまとまりのある英文で答えることが重要である。同意する／しない→理由・根拠→結論という流れで答えるとよい。

- No. 4はカードのトピックをさらに広い視点で捉えたうえでの質問。まずは質問の前に提供される話題を正しく理解することが重要。No. 2，3同様に理論的に意見をまとめよう。

# 準1級でよく出る文法

## 準1級レベルの文法

ここでは，準1級の文法問題や英文読解に必要な文法事項の基本を確認します。効率的に学習することができるよう，設問形式別にまとめてあります。

※付属の赤シートで答えを隠して取り組みましょう。

●語句選択補充問題 ——（　　）に適するものを選びましょう。

**1** 高速道路を運転するのは避けた方が良い。混雑しているだろう。

We should avoid （　③　） on the expressway.  It will be crowded.

① to drive 　　② drive 　　③ driving 　　④ to driving

**解説** avoidは動名詞を目的語にとる。

**2** その男は多くの人々に店から逃げて行くところを見られた。

The man was （　①　） away from the shop by many people.

① seen running 　② seeing to run 　③ seen run 　④ seeing running

**解説** 知覚動詞seeを受動態で使った文。

**3** あなたがここに着くころには，私たちは夕食を終えているだろう。

We will （　④　） dinner by the time you arrive here.

① be eaten 　　② be eating 　　③ be finished 　　④ have finished

**解説** 未来完了の文。

**4** 私は空港に着くとすぐに母に電話をかけた。

（　②　） at the airport, I called my mother.

① In arriving 　② Upon arriving 　③ With arriving 　④ Arriving

**解説** 〈upon＋動名詞〉「～するとすぐに」。

**5** 劇場でおじに会うとはまったく思わなかった。

（　④　） I would meet my uncle at the theater.

① Had not I thought 　　　　② Not I had thought

③ Never I had thought 　　　④ Never had I thought

**解説** 倒置の文。

**6** この問題について，信頼できる人なら誰にでも相談した方がよい。

You should consult （　②　） about this problem.

① whoever to trust 　　　　② whomever you trust

③ whoever trusted 　　　　④ whomever to be trusted

**解説** 目的格の複合関係代名詞。

**7** 彼女がもう少し早く起きていれば始発電車に乗れただろうに。

If she （　②　） up a little earlier, she （　②　） the first train.

① had gotten, could caught　　　② had gotten, could have caught

③ got, had caught　　　④ got, could have caught

**解説** 仮定法過去完了の文。

**8** 締め切りが近づいているので，今夜は眠る時間がほとんどない。

（　①　） the deadline （　①　）, I have little time to sleep tonight.

① With, approaching　　　② With, approach

③ On, approaching　　　④ On, approached

**解説** 付帯状況を表す with。

**9** あなたと同じように，私もテレビドラマには興味がない。

I'm not interested in TV dramas （　④　） than you are.

① no more　　② much less　　③ no less　　④ any more

**解説** not ～ any more than ... 「～でないのは…でないのと同じ」。

**10** 私が帰宅するまでに部屋は掃除されていなかった。

The room （　②　） by the time I got home.

① was not been cleaned　　　② had not been cleaned

③ has not cleaned　　　④ had never got cleaning

**解説** 受動態の過去完了。

**11** マイクはどんな仕事に就けばよいのかわからないで困っています。あなたが彼の父親だとしたら，彼にどうするように助言しますか。

Mike is at a loss as to what career to pursue. （　③　） that you were his father, what （　③　） you advise him to do?

① If, will　　　② If, would

③ Suppose, would　　　④ Suppose, will

**解説** 仮定法過去の文。Suppose that ～ ＝ If ～

**12** 私は父の故郷について聞かれて何も言うことができなかった。

I could not say anything （　②　） about the hometown of my father.

① when questioning　　　② when questioned

③ though I questioned　　　④ though questioning

**解説** 接続詞の後の〈S ＋ V〉(I was) が省略された文。

**1** 私はパスポートを更新してもらう必要がある。

I need to get my passport ( **renewed** ).

**解説** 〈get＋O＋過去分詞〉「Oを〜してもらう」。

**2** この夏は数週間雨が降らず，多くの植物が枯れる原因となった。

We had no rain for several weeks this summer, ( **causing** ) many plants to die.

**解説** 結果を表す分詞構文。

**3** 彼女には息子が２人いて，その１人はプロ野球チームの一員だ。

She has two sons, ( **one** ) ( **of** ) ( **whom** ) is a member of a professional baseball team.

**解説** 非制限用法の関係代名詞。

**4** 旅行に行くのに朝早く家を出たので，私たちは予想していたよりも多くの場所を訪れることができた。

( **Having** ) ( **left** ) home for the trip early in the morning, we were able to visit more places than we had expected.

**解説** 完了形の分詞構文。

**5** 父は，私が高校を卒業したら留学することを許してくれた。

My father allowed ( **me** ) ( **to** ) ( **study** ) abroad after I graduated from high school.

**解説** 〈allow＋O＋to *do*〉「Oが〜するのを許可する」。

**6** 誰が来ようともドアを開けてはいけない。

Don't open the door ( **whoever** ) ( **comes** ).

**解説** 主格の複合関係代名詞。

**7** 私はあなたが駅に着くまで20分くらい待っていた。

I ( **had** ) ( **been** ) ( **waiting** ) for you for about 20 minutes when you arrived at the station.

**解説** 過去完了進行形。

**8** 息子は熱がある。だから釣りには行かせないよ。

My son has a fever. That's ( **why** ) I won't let him go fishing.

**解説** That's why 〜 「そういうわけで〜，だから〜」。

**9** 私はそのレストランに行くといつもスパゲッティーを食べる。

I eat spaghetti at that restaurant ( **whenever** ) ( **I** ) ( **go** ) there.

**解説** whenever 「〜するときはいつでも」。

**10** そのアメリカ人の歌手が流ちょうな日本語でスピーチをして，私たちは大いに驚いた。

The American singer made a speech in fluent Japanese, ( **which** ) surprised us very much.

**解説** 非制限用法の関係代名詞。

**11** 子供たちを起こさないように静かに部屋に入ってね。

Go into the room quietly ( **so** ) ( **that** ) you might not wake the children.

**解説** 目的を表すso that。

**12** もう一度パリへ行ったら，私は3回そこに行ったことになる。

If I go to Paris again, I ( **will** ) ( **have** ) ( **been** ) there three times.

**解説** 未来完了の文。

**13** 姉はたとえ勉強で忙しくても，私を車で駅まで連れて行ってくれた。

My sister drove me to the station, ( **even** ) ( **though** ) she was busy with her studies.

**解説** even thoughの後には事実が続く。

**14** 調査に基づくと，この村の人口はこの10年間で30パーセント減少した。

( **Based** ) ( **on** ) research, the population of this village has decreased 30 percent over the past ten years.

**解説** 過去分詞で始まる分詞構文。

**15** この規則が適用されない例外的なケースがいくつかある。

There are some exceptional cases ( **in** ) ( **which** ) this rule does not apply.

**解説** 〈前置詞＋関係代名詞〉。

**16** その国の言葉についてほとんど理解していなかったけれども，少女は何とかそこの人々とうまくやっていくことができた。

( **Though** ) (understanding) little about the language of the country, the girl managed to get along with the people there.

**解説** 接続詞を伴う分詞構文。

**17** たとえ彼にお金がたくさんあったとしても，彼は生き方を変えないだろう。

( **Even** ) ( **if** ) he had a lot of money, he would not change his life-style.

**解説** 仮定法過去の文。even ifの後には事実に反する内容が続く。

**18** 幹線道路でひどい自動車事故が起こったことが明らかになった。

（　　**It**　　）became clear（　　**that**　　）a terrible car accident had happened on the highway.

**解説** that以下を受ける形式主語のit。

**19** もう試験は終わったのだから，休暇の計画でも立てよう。

（　　**Now**　　）（　　**that**　　）the exam is over, I'll plan my vacation.

**解説** now that「（今は）～なのだから」。

**20** とても寒かったが，ボランティアたちは朝早く災害現場へ出て行った。

（　　**It**　　）（　　**being**　　）very cold, the volunteers went out to the disaster site early in the morning.

**解説** 独立分詞構文。

**21** 彼と話して初めて，彼がいかに知的であるかがわかった。

（　　**Not**　　）（　　**until**　　）I talked with him（　　**did**　　）I realize how intelligent he was.

**解説** 倒置の文。

**22** 天気予報を調べておくんだった。

I（　　**should**　　）（　　**have**　　）checked the weather forecast.

**解説** 〈should have ＋過去分詞〉後悔を表す。

---

●**語句整序問題**──（　　）内の語句を正しく並べかえましょう。

※（　　）の中では，文のはじめにくる語も小文字になっています。

**1** 火事のせいで森の半分が消滅した。

The fire ( to / half / disappear / the forest / caused / of ).

**解答** caused half of the forest to disappear　**解説** 〈cause＋O＋to *do*〉「Oに～させる［Oが～する原因となる］」。

**2** どうしてあなたはあんな失礼な振る舞いができるの？

( you / rude / behave / in / could / a / how / such ) way?

**解答** How could you behave in such a rude　**解説** 反語表現の文。

**3** 彼は月に50冊も本を読む。

He ( books / less / month / than / reads / fifty / no / a ).

**解答** reads no less than fifty books a month　**解説** no less than ～「～ほども多くの」。

**4** 電車の遅延のせいで，そこに着くには本来の３倍の時間がかかるだろう。

( times / as / take / there / long / to / will / three / as / it / get ) it should because of the train delay.

**解答** It will take three times as long to get there as　**解説** It takes ～「（時間が）～かかる」。～ times as ... as ─「─の～倍…」。

**5** 私たちが乗る飛行機は嵐のために遅れると予測されている。

Our plane ( delayed / of / is / to / because / expected / be ) the storm.

**解答** is expected to be delayed because of **解説** 〈expect＋O＋to *do*〉「Oが〜すると予期［期待］する」を受動態で使った文。

**6** この庭園では多くの種類の花が栽培されているのを見ることができる。

We can ( kinds / grown / many / of / flowers / see / being ) in this garden.

**解答** see many kinds of flowers being grown **解説** 〈see＋O＋現在分詞〉「Oが〜しているのを見る」。being grownは受け身の形。

**7** あなたの支援がなかったら，この計画は失敗していただろう。

( support / not / it / your / had / for / been ), this project would have failed.

**解答** Had it not been for your support **解説** 仮定法過去完了の倒置文。

**8** 湖にはほとんど水が残っていなかったので，村の人々は雨乞いをした。

( left / being / the lake / little / there / in / water ), people in the village prayed for rain.

**解答** There being little water left in the lake **解説** There is 〜構文の分詞構文。

**9** 私は犬が小川を泳いで渡るのを見た。

I ( across / small / swim / a dog / river / saw / a ).

**解答** saw a dog swim across a small river **解説** 〈see＋O＋動詞の原形〉「Oが〜するのを見る」。

**10** あなたのいなくなった猫はどのような見た目なのか教えてください。

Please tell ( cat / like / what / me / missing / looks / your ).

**解答** me what your missing cat looks like **解説** 間接疑問文。

**11** ジョンはアジアの国々へ旅行することを考えていたが，彼の父親の病気のために旅行することができなくなった。

John was thinking of traveling to some Asian countries, but ( for / made / his / travel / illness / impossible / it / him / father's / to ).

**解答** his father's illness made it impossible for him to travel **解説** 無生物主語の文。itは形式的な目的語。

**12** 私は両親に，その大学に入学するには相当な努力が必要だと言われた。

I was told by my parents that ( of / would / to / accepted / take / a lot / it / effort / be ) by that college.

**解答** it would take a lot of effort to be accepted **解説** itは形式主語。

**13** あなたが私の立場だったらどうしているだろうか。

( doing / were / be / if / you / what / would / in / you ) my place?

**解答** What would you be doing if you were in **解説** 仮定法過去の文。

# 準1級でよく出るイディ

## 準1級レベルのイディオム

ここでは，準1級でよく出るイディオムを集めました。効率的に学習できるよう，文の中での使い方を覚えられる例文形式で紹介しています。

日本文の意味を表す英文になるように，（　　）に適する英語を入れましょう。

※付属の赤シートで答えを隠して取り組みましょう。

### 名詞を含むイディオム

**1.** We ( **took** ) ( **advantage** ) ( **of** ) the good weather to enjoy cycling.
私たちは好天気を利用してサイクリングを楽しんだ。

**2.** The reconstruction of the castle will ( **give** ) the local economy a ( **boost** ).
その城の再建は地元経済に活気を与えるだろう。

**3.** Buying daily necessities ( **in** ) ( **bulk** ) allows you a bit of savings.
日用品をまとめ買いすれば，ちょっとしたお金の節約につながる。

**4.** Using a spell-checking tool saves you a ( **bundle** ) ( **of** ) time.
スペルチェックの機能を使えば，多くの［大幅に］時間を節約できる。

**5.** The hurricane did devastating ( **damage** ) ( **to** ) the coastal areas.
そのハリケーンは沿岸地域に壊滅的な被害をもたらした。

**6.** These days, many families are struggling to ( **make** ) ( **ends** ) ( **meet** ).
最近では，多くの家庭が家計をやりくりするのに四苦八苦している。

**7.** Sarah was brought ( **face** ) ( **to** ) ( **face** ) with the horrors of war.
サラは戦争の恐ろしさに直面した。

**8.** Larry will ( **land** ) ( **on** ) his ( **feet** ) whatever happens to him.
何事が起ころうとも，ラリーはきっとうまく切り抜けるだろう。

**9.** Kate didn't want to ( **make** ) a ( **fuss** ) over nothing.
ケイトはつまらないことで騒ぎ立てたくなかった。

10. You should ( **have** ) ( **a** ) ( **go** ) at fishing in mountain streams.
    ぜひ渓流釣りをやってみるべきだよ。

11. Skipping meals to lose weight ( **does** ) ( **harm** ) to your health.
    減量のために食事を抜くことは健康に悪影響を及ぼす。

12. You need something to take your ( **mind** ) ( **off** ) work.
    あなたには何か仕事を忘れさせてくれるものが必要ですよ。

13. These days, many companies allow workers to ( **take** ) a ( **nap** ).
    最近では，多くの会社が社員に昼寝をすることを許可している。

14. That noise really gets ( **on** ) my ( **nerves** ).
    あの騒音は本当に神経に障る。

15. We're running out of time, so you should ( **stick** ) ( **to** ) the point.
    時間がないので，問題点からそれないようにお願いします。

16. Social unrest sometimes ( **gives** ) ( **rise** ) to riots.
    社会不安は時として暴動を引き起こす。

17. Running every day is one of the best ways to get ( **in** ) ( **shape** ).
    毎日ジョギングすることは体を鍛えるのに最も良い方法の１つだ。

18. George always takes ( **sides** ) ( **with** ) his sister.
    ジョージはいつも妹の味方をする［肩を持つ］。

19. The police officer ( **lost** ) ( **sight** ) of the suspect in the crowd.
    警官は人混みの中で容疑者を見失った。

20. The airliner came to a ( **full** ) ( **stop** ) at the gate.
    旅客機はゲートのところで完全に停止した。

21. Our boss often ( **loses** ) his ( **temper** ) over trivial things.
    私たちの上司はよくささいなことでカッとなる）。

22. The drought ( **took** ) a heavy ( **toll** ) on crops.
    干ばつで農作物に大きな被害が出た。

23. Please get ( **in** ) ( **touch** ) ( **with** ) us right away if you have a problem.
    問題があれば，すぐに私たちに連絡してください。

**24.** Peter keeps ( **in** ) ( **touch** ) with his family by phone.
ピーターは電話で家族と絶えず連絡を取り合っている。

**25.** Terry walks every morning ( **with** ) a ( **view** ) to improving his health.
テリーは健康を増進する目的で毎朝散歩している。

## 動詞を含むイディオム①

**1.** Coffee ( **accounts** ) ( **for** ) more than 10% of the country's export revenue.
コーヒーはその国の輸出収入の10パーセント以上を占めている。

**2.** The total development cost ( **added** ) ( **up** ) to 50 million dollars.
開発費の総額は5,000万ドルに上った。

**3.** Many people ( **associate** ) Canada ( **with** ) maple syrup.
多くの人々はカナダと聞くとメープルシロップを連想する。

**4.** The party leader refused to ( **back** ) ( **down** ) his comments on the refugee issue.
その党首は難民問題に関する彼の発言を撤回するのを拒んだ。

**5.** We should ( **back** ) ( **off** ) and let Andy make his own decision.
私たちは口出し［干渉］をやめて，アンディに自分で決めさせるべきだよ。

**6.** Anne is a bit nervous before an important game. Just ( **bear** ) ( **with** ) her.
アンは大事な試合の前で少し緊張しているの。大目に見てあげてちょうだい。

**7.** Negotiations between the two countries ( **broke** ) ( **down** ).
その2国間の交渉は決裂した。

**8.** A fire ( **broke** ) ( **out** ) downtown and destroyed several stores.
繁華街で火災が起きて，いくつかの店が焼けた。

**9.** The bribery scandal may ( **bring** ) ( **down** ) the minister.
その贈収賄事件は大臣をその座から引きずり下ろすかもしれない。

**10.** The idea of outsourcing some work was ( **brought** ) ( **up** ) at the meeting.
会議では作業の一部を外注する案が提出された。

**11.** I know you're busy, but be careful not to (　　**burn**　　) (　　**out**　　).
忙しいのはわかるが，くれぐれも燃え尽きないように注意してね。

**12.** A bomb disposal team was (　　**called**　　) (　　**in**　　) to deal with a suspicious package.
不審な荷物を処理するために爆弾処理班が呼ばれた。

**13.** The fireworks were (　　**called**　　) (　　**off**　　) because of rain.
雨のため，花火大会は中止になった。

**14.** Don't get (　　**carried**　　) (　　**away**　　) and spend too much money.
あまり調子に乗ってお金を使いすぎないようにね。

**15.** Mike didn't (　　**catch**　　) (　　**on**　　) to what was going on.
マイクには何が起きているのか理解（することが）できなかった。

**16.** John had to work hard to (　　**catch**　　) (　　**up**　　) on his studies.
ジョンは勉強の遅れを取り戻すのに必死に勉強しなければならなかった。

**17.** Let's (　　**check**　　) (　　**out**　　) the lowest price of the camera on the Internet.
そのカメラの最安値をネットで調べよう。

**18.** Bill and Judy (　　**chipped**　　) (　　**in**　　) to buy their father a tie.
ビルとジュディーはお金を出し合って父親にネクタイを買ってあげた。

**19.** How's your history report (　　**coming**　　) (　　**along**　　)?
歴史のレポートの進み具合はどう？

**20.** Sarah (　　**came**　　) (　　**down**　　) with the flu the day before her trip.
サラは旅行に行く前日にインフルエンザにかかってしまった。

**21.** The new printer (　　**comes**　　) (　　**in**　　) three colors —— white, red, and black.
この新しいプリンターは白，赤，黒の3色がそろっている。

**22.** Lucy (　　**came**　　) (　　**into**　　) a large amount of money after her grandmother died.
祖母が亡くなったあと，ルーシーは莫大なお金を相続した。

**23.** All we can do now is wait and see how things (　　**come**　　) (　　**out**　　).
今私たちにできるのは事態がどうなるか見守ることだけだ。

**24.** Why don't you (　　**come**　　) (　　**over**　　) to my house this afternoon?
今日の午後，僕の家に（遊びに）来ませんか？

**25.** Eating high-calorie fast food every day （ **contributes** ）（ **to** ） obesity.

高カロリーのファースフードを毎日食べることは肥満の原因となる。

**26.** Ralph is someone you can （ **count** ）（ **on** ） in time of need.

ラルフはいざという時に頼りにできる人だ。

**27.** Alan （ **covered** ）（ **for** ） Helen while she was on vacation.

ヘレンが休暇をとっている間，アランが彼女の代わりを務めた。

**28.** Energy-saving air conditioners will help （ **cut** ）（ **back** ） on electricity bills.

省エネ型のエアコンは電気代を節約する助けとなるでしょう。


## 動詞を含むイディオム②

**1.** I just can't afford to （ **dish** ）（ **out** ） $2,000 for replacing computers.

コンピュータの買い換えに２千ドルも出費する余裕はない。

**2.** You should not （ **drag** ） your children （ **into** ） adult affairs.

子供たちを大人の事情に巻き込むべきではない。

**3.** The sales meeting （ **dragged** ）（ **on** ） for hours.

営業会議は何時間も延々と続いた。

**4.** His presentation was good, but he （ **dragged** ） it （ **out** ） a bit too long.

彼の発表はよかったが，彼は少し長々と引っ張りすぎた。

**5.** Jack didn't want to get （ **drawn** ）（ **into** ） their arguments, so he kept silent.

ジャックは彼らの議論に巻き込まれたくなかったので，黙っていた。

**6.** Abel （ **drew** ）（ **on** ） his knowledge of the law to write the courtroom mystery.

アベルは法律に関する知識を活用して，その法廷ミステリーを書いた。

**7.** As the financial resources （ **dried** ）（ **up** ）, the project failed halfway.

財源が枯渇したため，その計画は途中で行き詰まった。

**8.** Adam has some savings in the bank to （ **fall** ）（ **back** ） on in an emergency.

アダムはいざという時に当てにできる預金が銀行に少しある。

9. Sam almost ( **fell** ) ( **for** ) the salesperson's smooth talk.
サムはもう少しでセールスマンのうまい話に引っかかるところだった。

10. The responsibility for caring for his aging parents ( **fell** ) ( **on** ) his shoulders.
年老いた両親の介護の責任が彼の肩にのしかかった。

11. The construction plan ( **fell** ) ( **through** ) due to local objection.
その建設計画は地元住民の反対で失敗に終わった。

12. Brian tried to ( **figure** ) ( **out** ) what's wrong with his microwave.
ブライアンは彼の電子レンジのどこが悪いのか突き止めようとした。

13. Could you ( **fill** ) ( **in** ) for me at the meeting this afternoon?
今日の午後の会議，私の代わりに出ていただけますか。

14. You just need to ( **fill** ) ( **out** ) this application form to register.
登録するにはこの申し込み用紙に記入するだけでよいのです。

15. The restaurant ( **fills** ) ( **up** ) quickly after six every evening.
そのレストランは毎晩6時を過ぎるとすぐに一杯になる。

16. Now many manufacturers are ( **focusing** ) ( **on** ) reducing the cost.
今や多くのメーカーはコスト削減に集中している。

17. Thomas finally got ( **around** ) ( **to** ) rearranging his room last weekend.
先週末になってトーマスはようやく部屋の模様替えをする時間がとれた。

18. Alice tried to ( **get** ) ( **at** ) the truth about the case.
アリスはその事件の真相を突き止めようとした。

19. Nobody will ( **get** ) ( **away** ) with such a serious crime.
このような重大な犯罪を犯して逃げおおせる者などだれもいない。

20. I don't think I can ( **get** ) ( **by** ) without using the Internet.
インターネットを使わずにやっていけるとは思えません。

21. The roof of the warehouse ( **gave** ) ( **in** ) under the weight of the snow.
倉庫の屋根は雪の重みで壊れた。

**22.** The factory management finally ( **gave** ) ( **in** ) ( **to** ) the workers' demand.
工場の経営者側はついに労働者たちの要求に屈した。

**23.** Nuclear waste continues to ( **give** ) ( **off** ) harmful radiation.
放射性廃棄物は人体に有害な放射線を放出し続ける。

**24.** I guess we have to ( **go** ) ( **along** ) with the president's decision.
私たちは社長の決定に従うしかなさそうだ。

**25.** I think I'll ( **go** ) ( **for** ) this tuna salad sandwiches.
私はこのツナサラダサンドイッチにしようと思います。

**26.** ( **Go** ) ( **over** ) your report once again before you hand it in.
提出する前にもう一度レポートを見直しなさい。

**27.** Ron's family ( **went** ) ( **through** ) several hurricanes over the last two years.
ロンの家族はこの２年間に数回のハリケーンを経験した。

**28.** The committee ( **hammered** ) ( **out** ) a solution to the issue.
委員会はその問題に対する解決策を打ち出した。

**29.** Mary took a shower before ( **heading** ) ( **off** ) to work.
メアリーは仕事に出かける前にシャワーを浴びた。

## 動詞を含むイディオム③

**1.** Katie struggled to ( **hold** ) ( **back** ) her tears.
ケイティーは必死に涙をこらえようとした。

**2.** Randy ( **held** ) ( **off** ) making a decision on the matter.
ランディはその件に関して決断するのを先延ばしにした。

**3.** The boy managed to ( **hold** ) ( **on** ) without food for three days.
その少年は３日間食べ物なしで何とか持ちこたえた。

**4.** Their food supplies won't ( **hold** ) ( **out** ) for another week.
彼らの食料はあと１週間はもたないだろう。

**5.** Frank ( **jumped** ) ( **at** ) the opportunity to try the product out for free.
フランクは無料でその製品を試すことができる機会に飛びついた。

6. Paul had difficulties ( **keeping** ) ( **up** ) at school.
ポールは学校で勉強についていくのが難しかった。

7. It is not easy for us to ( **keep** ) ( **up** )
( **with** ) world affairs.
私たちにとって世界情勢に遅れずについて行くことは簡単なことではない。

8. They ( **kicked** ) ( **off** ) the celebration event with a parade.
その祝賀イベントはパレードで始まった。

9. The old apartment house is going to be ( **knocked** ) ( **down** ).
その古いアパートは取り壊されることになっている。

10. The school ( **laid** ) ( **down** ) strict rules about the use of smartphone.
その学校はスマートフォンの使用に関する厳しい規則を定めた。

11. The factory was forced to ( **lay** ) ( **off** ) hundreds of workers.
その工場では何百人もの従業員を解雇する事態に追い込まれた。

12. You said you could meet the deadline. Don't ( **let** ) me ( **down** ).
締め切りには間に合うと言ったじゃないか。がっかりさせないでくれよ。

13. If we ( **let** ) ( **up** ) now, all our efforts could come to nothing.
ここで気を抜いたら，私たちの努力はすべて水の泡になるでしょう。

14. Alan stopped trying to ( **live** ) ( **up** ) to his parents' expectations.
アランは両親の期待に応えようと努力することをやめた。

15. Sarah is ( **looking** ) ( **into** ) doing some volunteer work on her days off.
サラは休みの日にボランティアの仕事をすることを検討している。

16. The sign reads, "( **Look** ) out ( **for** ) falling rocks."
その標識には「落石に注意せよ」と書かれている。

17. Some consumers feel the economy is ( **looking** ) ( **up** ).
経済が上向いていると感じている消費者もいる。

18. You'll ( **make** ) ( **it** ) on time for the train if you take a taxi.
タクシーを使えば列車に間に合いますよ。

19. Bill simply couldn't ( **make** ) ( **out** ) what his boss said.
ビルは上司の言うことを全く理解することができなかった。

**20.** Keith is struggling to ( **make** ) ( **up** )
( **for** ) lost time.
キースは時間の遅れを取り戻そうと必死になっている。

**21.** The art exhibition didn't ( **measure** ) ( **up** ) to her
expectations.
その美術展は彼女の期待に沿うものではなかった。

**22.** The company ( **passed** ) ( **off** ) imported beef as
domestic beef.
その会社は輸入牛肉を国産とごまかした。

**23.** Tom looked dissatisfied because he got ( **passed** ) ( **over** )
for a promotion.
トムは昇進が見送られて憮然とした表情だった。

**24.** I can't believe Brian ( **passed** ) ( **up** ) such a good offer.
ブライアンがあのような良いオファーを見送ったなんて信じられない。

**25.** The group ( **pushed** ) ( **for** ) a ban on smoking in public
places.
そのグループは公共の場所での喫煙禁止を強く求めた。

**26.** They ( **put** ) ( **forward** ) a plan for promoting e-learning
in public schools.
彼らは公立学校におけるeラーニング奨励の計画を提出した。

**27.** The police have not ( **ruled** ) ( **out** ) the possibility of
terrorism.
警察はテロの可能性を排除していない。

**28.** I want to ( **take** ) ( **in** ) a musical during my stay in
New York.
ニューヨーク滞在中にミュージカルを見に行きたい。

**29.** The restaurant was full, so the staff had to ( **turn** )
( **away** ) customers.
レストランは満席だったので，係員は客の入店を断らねばならなかった。

**30.** Engineers have ( **worked** ) ( **out** ) some issues with the
new airliner.
技術者たちはその新型の旅客機のいくつかの問題点を解決した。

## 形容詞を含むイディオム

**1.** Russia is ( **abundant** ) ( **in** ) natural resources.
ロシアは天然資源が豊富である。

2. Julia is（ **apt** ）（ **to** ） believe easily what the mass media tells.
   ジュリアはマスコミの言うことを簡単に信じる傾向がある。
3. They are（ **committed** ）（ **to** ） fighting against poverty in developing countries.
   彼らは開発途上国における貧困との戦いに献身的に取り組んでいる。
4. Many people are（ **concerned** ）（ **about** ） the safety of food.
   多くの人々は食品の安全を心配している。
5. The results of the experiment are（ **consistent** ）（ **with** ） our hypothesis.
   実験結果は私たちの仮説と一致している。
6. All exchange students are （ **exempt** ）（ **from** ） paying tuition fees.
   交換留学生は授業料の支払いを免除される。
7. The Christmas event is（ **geared** ）（ **toward** ） children.
   そのクリスマスのイベントは子供が対象である。
8. The company（ **went** ）（ **bankrupt** ） due to massive debt.
   その会社は巨額の負債を抱えて倒産した。
9. We're（ **grateful** ）（ **for** ） your most generous support in the past.
   私たちはあなたのこれまでの絶大なるご支援に感謝いたします。
10. Many people are（ **ignorant** ）（ **of** ） the beauty of nature on the island.
    多くの人々はその島の自然の美しさを知らない。
11. The falling unemployment rate is（ **indicative** ）（ **of** ） an improving economy.
    失業率の減少は経済が回復に向かっていることを示している。
12. The Internet is（ **indispensable** ）（ **to** ） our daily life.
    インターネットは私たちの日常生活に欠かせない。
13. The boy is（ **liable** ）（ **to** ） respiratory diseases.
    その男の子は呼吸器系の病気にかかりやすい。
14. Miyuki is（ **particular** ）（ **about** ） her food.
    ミユキは食べ物の好みがうるさい。
15. Oliver was（ **reluctant** ）（ **to** ） talk about his past.
    オリバーは自分の過去について話すのを嫌がった。

## 前置詞を含むイディオム

**1.** The engineer worked ( **around** ) the ( **clock** ) to fix the problem.
その技師はその問題を解決するために24時間ぶっ通しで働いた。

**2.** We must make this event a success ( **at** ) ( **all** ) ( **costs** ).
私たちはなんとしてもこのイベントを成功させなければならない。

**3.** You must hand in your report by October 14th ( **at** ) the ( **latest** ).
レポートは遅くとも10月14日までに提出しなければなりません。

**4.** In many cases, invasive species are introduced ( **by** ) ( **accident** ).
多くの場合，侵入生物種は偶然持ち込まれる。

**5.** Fred didn't turn up for the meetings three times ( **in** ) a ( **row** ).
フレッドは3回連続してミーティングに姿を見せなかった。

**6.** Most local residents are ( **in** ) ( **favor** ) ( **of** ) the construction of the railroad.
地域住民の大部分はその鉄道の建設に賛成している。

**7.** ( **In** ) ( **terms** ) ( **of** ) service quality, the hotel was excellent.
サービスの質に関してはそのホテルは申し分なかった。

**8.** The pamphlet shows us what to do ( **in** ) the ( **event** ) ( **of** ) an earthquake.
この小冊子は地震の際に私たちがどうすべきかを教えてくれる。

**9.** The twin sisters looked after their puppy ( **in** ) ( **turn** ).
その双子の姉妹は自分たちの子犬を交替で世話した。

**10.** Keith tried ( **in** ) ( **vain** ) to track down his old friend.
キースは古い友人を見つけ出そうとしたがだめだった。

**11.** The popularity of the rock band is ( **on** ) the ( **rise** ) around the world.
そのロックバンドは世界中で人気が上昇中だ。

**12.** Scott turned down the offer ( **on** ) the ( **spot** ).
スコットはその場でその申し出を断った。

**13.** Many plant and animal species are ( **on** ) the ( **verge** ) ( **of** ) extinction.
多くの植物種や動物種が絶滅の危機に瀕している。

# 準1級レベルの口語表現

リスニング問題のPart1と3，また筆記の大問1では，日常生活やビジネススシーンで使われる決まり文句，口語表現が多数出てくるのが特徴です。場面ごとに頻出の英文をチェックしておきましょう。

日本文の意味を表す英文になるように，（　　）に適する英語を入れましょう。

※付属の赤シートで答えを隠して取り組みましょう。

## あいさつ

1. Oh, it's Bruce! ( **Long** ) ( **time** ) no ( **see** ). How's life?
   —— ( **Looking** ) up. I got a promotion to the sales manager last month.
   まあ，ブルースじゃないの。久しぶりね。調子はどう？
   —— 上向いてきているよ。先月営業部長に昇進したんだ。

2. Thanks for calling Iris Bookstore. ( **How** ) may I help ( **you** )?
   —— Hello, I'm calling about my order I made ten days ago.
   アイリス書店にお電話をいただき，ありがとうございます。ご用件を承ります。
   —— もしもし，10日前に注文した品物のことでお電話したのですが。

3. I'll check your order status and call you back later.
   —— I'd really ( **appreciate** ) that.
   お客様のご注文の状況を調べて，後ほどこちらからお電話いたします。
   —— それは非常に助かります。

4. ( **How** ) are you ( **feeling** ) this morning, Kate? Is your cold any better?
   —— ( **Much** ) ( **better** ) than yesterday, thanks.
   ケイト，今朝の気分はどうだい？　風邪は少しはよくなった？
   —— 昨日よりはずっと気分がいいわ。ありがとう。

5. ( **It** ) was great ( **to** ) see you, Sophie.
   —— You ( **too** )\*. See you again, Randy.
   ソフィー，お会いできてうれしかったよ。
   —— 私もよ。また会いましょう，ランディ。

\* You too. = It was great to see <u>you, too</u>.

37

## 許可を求める・依頼する

**6.** Would you ( **mind** ) ( **my[me]** ) smoking here?
—— No, ( **not** ) at ( **all** ) . /
I'd rather ( **you** ) ( **didn't** ) .
ここでたばこを吸ってもいいですか。
—— かまいませんよ。/ 吸わないでくださるとうれしいです。

**7.** Mr. Hawkins, would you ( **mind** ) sparing a few minutes?
—— Sure. What is it? /
I'm sorry, but I'm ( **tied** ) ( **up** ) at the moment.
ホーキンスさん，少しお時間をいただけますでしょうか。
—— いいとも。なんだい？/ 申し訳ないが，今手が離せないんだ。

**8.** I have a ( **favor** ) to ( **ask** ), honey. Could you pick me
up at the station?
—— No ( **problem** ) . I'll be there in fifteen minutes.
あなた，お願いがあるの。駅まで車で迎えに来てくれないかしら。
—— いいよ。15分でそちらへ行くから。

**9.** Ms. Ellen, I was ( **wondering** ) ( **if** ) you ( **could** )
give me advice. —— I'm always ready to help you. ( **What's** ) up?
エレン先生，アドバイスをいただけませんでしょうか。
—— いつでも力になるわよ。どうしたの？

## 勧誘・提案する

**10.** Would you ( **care** ) for some hot drinks?
—— Yes, I'd ( **like** ) some tea.
何か温かい飲み物はいかがですか。—— はい，紅茶をいただきます。

**11.** If you're free this afternoon, why ( **not** ) go shopping with me?
—— In this rain? I'd ( **rather** ) stay at home and read a book.
今日の午後暇なら，一緒に買い物に行かない？
—— こんな雨の中をかい？ 僕は家にいて本を読む方がいいや。

**12.** How ( **about** ) ( **letting** ) Bill organize the event? I think
he's suited for that kind of job. —— Maybe you're ( **right** ) .
そのイベント，ビルに企画を任せたらどうかしら。そういう仕事に彼は適任
だと思うわ。—— 君の言う通りかもしれない。

**13.** Why ( **don't** ) ( **we** ) order some pizza tonight?
—— I'm ( **for** ) that. I'm too exhausted to make dinner.
今夜はピザを取らないか？
—— 賛成よ。くたくたで夕食を作る気力もないわ。

**14.** I ( **was** ) ( **wondering** ) ( **if** ) you'd like to join our party next Sunday.

—— That's sweet ( **of** ) ( **you** ), but I'm booked that day.

今度の日曜日，私たちのパーティーにいらっしゃいませんか。

—— ご親切にありがとうございます。でも，その日は別の約束があるのです。

**15.** Why ( **don't** ) ( **you** ) try to sell your unwanted items through an online auction?

—— Oh, I didn't think of that. It may be worth a try.

不要品をネットオークションで売ってみたらどう？

—— それは考えてもいなかったよ。試してみる価値はあるかもね。

### 意見・感想を求める

**16.** How ( **was** ) the new theme park? —— We ( **found** ) it highly amusing! It has loads of attractions for kids.

新しいテーマパークはどうだった？ —— とてもおもしろかったよ。子供向けのアトラクションがたくさんあってね。

**17.** How are you ( **getting** ) ( **along** ) ( **with** ) your dorm roommate?

—— Yes, he's a very friendly guy. He's a little messy, though.

寮のルームメイトとはうまくやっているの？

—— うん，とても気さくなやつだよ。ちょっと散らかし屋だけどね。

### 相手をほめる・評価する・励ます

**18.** I've just been promoted to sales manager.

—— (**Congratulations**)！ This calls for a celebration.

たった今，営業部長に昇進が決まったの。

—— おめでとう！ これはお祝いをしなくちゃね。

**19.** Mr. Robert, I've just finished all the documents for tomorrow's meeting.

—— You ( **made** ) ( **it** ), Emily!

ロバートさん，ちょうど明日の会議のための資料を全部作り終えました。

—— やったじゃないか，エミリー。

**20.** I don't think we can finish this job by five, Peter.

—— ( **Hang** ) ( **in** ) there, Mary. We're almost done.

この仕事，5時までに終えられそうにないわ，ピーター。

—— がんばれ，メアリー。もうほとんど終わりかけているじゃないか。

## 申し出る・勧める・忠告する

**21.** Please （　**feel**　）（　**free**　）（　**to**　）call me when you're in trouble.

 —— That's very kind of you.  I'll be （　**counting**　）on you.

困ったときは，どうぞ遠慮なく電話してください。

 —— ご親切にどうもありがとう。頼りにしています。

**22.** Please don't （　**hesitate**　）（　**to**　）contact us if you have any questions.

質問があるときはどうぞご遠慮なくご連絡ください。

## 健康（病気・けが・薬）

**23.** It sounds like your cough is （　**hanging**　）（　**on**　）.  Are you OK? —— I think my asthma is （　**acting**　）（　**up**　）.  I'm going to see a doctor tomorrow.

君の咳，なかなか止まらないみたいだね。大丈夫かい？

 —— ぜんそくがまたひどくなっているみたいなの。明日医者に診てもらうわ。

**24.** My mother broke her leg last week, and she's （　**in**　）the （　**hospital**　）. —— Oh, （　**that's**　）too （　**bad**　）.  I hope she'll recover soon.

先週母が足の骨を折って，入院しているのです。

 —— それはお気の毒ですね。早く治るといいですね。

## 相づち・つなぎ言葉（談話標識）

**25.** What a coincidence, running into you at the art gallery!

 —— （　**Actually**　）, my sister's paintings are displayed here.

画廊であなたに会うなんて偶然ね！

 —— 実は姉の描いた絵がここに展示されているんだ。

**26.** Don't you like sweets, Kana? —— （　**On**　）the （　**contrary**　）.  I love them, but I'm on a diet now.

カナ，君は甘い物が好きじゃないの？

 —— とんでもないわ。大好きよ。でも，今ダイエット中なの。

**27.** Can I ask you to work overtime today, Anne?

 —— No （　**way**　）!  I have an appointment today.  Ask someone else.

今日残業をお願いできるかな，アン。

 —— お断りします［絶対に嫌です］。今日は用事があるのです。ほかの人に頼んでください。

# 準1級

## 2023年度 第2回

一次試験　2023.10.8実施

二次試験　A日程　2023.11.5実施
　　　　　B日程　2023.11.12実施
　　　　　C日程　2023.11.23実施

一次試験・筆記（90分）
　　　　　pp.42〜57

一次試験・リスニング（約31分）
　　　　　pp.58〜63
　　　　　CD青-1〜26

二次試験・面接（約8分）
　　　　　pp.64〜67

※解答一覧は別冊p.3
※解答と解説は別冊pp.4〜46

※別冊の巻末についている解答用マークシートを使いましょう。

## 合格基準スコア

- 一次試験……1792
　（満点2250／リーディング750, リスニング750, ライティング750）
- 二次試験……512（満点750／スピーキング750）

**1**

*To complete each item, choose the best word or phrase from among the four choices. Then, on your answer sheet, find the number of the question and mark your answer.*

*(1)* Layla found the workouts in the advanced class too (　　), so she decided to change to an easier class.

**1** subtle **2** contrary **3** strenuous **4** cautious

*(2)* The tax accountant asked the woman to (　　) all her financial records over the past year. He needed to see them before he could begin preparing her tax forms.

**1** punctuate **2** compile **3** bleach **4** obsess

*(3)* Emilio discovered a small leak in one of the water pipes in his house. To be safe, he turned off the (　　) to stop the water until he knew exactly what the problem was.

**1** depot **2** canal **3** valve **4** panel

*(4)* *A:* How long have you and Linda been (　　), Bill?
*B:* Oh, we've known each other for at least 10 years, maybe longer.

**1** acquainted **2** discharged **3** emphasized **4** subdued

*(5)* Our local community center usually has one main room, but when necessary, we can close the (　　) and create two smaller rooms.

**1** estimation **2** partition **3** assumption **4** notion

*(6)* Tyler's father suggested that he get some foreign (　　) from his local bank before his vacation because changing money abroad is often more expensive.

**1** tactic **2** bait **3** currency **4** menace

*(7)* Thanks to the country's (　　　) natural resources, it is able to earn a great deal of money through exports such as metals, coal, and natural gas.

**1** unjust **2** insubstantial **3** elastic **4** abundant

*(8)* At first, Enzo listed all six of his previous jobs on his résumé. He had to remove two of them, however, in order to (　　　) the document into one page.

**1** dispute **2** mumble **3** mistrust **4** condense

*(9)* In most countries, foreigners working without a proper visa are (　　　) if they are discovered. However, sending them home can cost a lot of money.

**1** mended **2** deported **3** perceived **4** distributed

*(10)* Tim is worried that he is spending too much time using his smartphone. He feels a strong (　　　) to check his e-mail every few minutes.

**1** suspension **2** extension **3** seclusion **4** compulsion

*(11)* *A:* Did you make a New Year's (　　　) this year, Serena?
*B:* Yes, I decided to start eating healthy snacks instead of sweets between meals. It's been difficult to keep away from the chocolate and candy, though.

**1** astonishment **2** resolution **3** vulnerability **4** repression

*(12)* Miranda noticed that the amount of money in her savings account was (　　　), so she decided to start spending less every month.

**1** grazing **2** dwindling **3** browsing **4** rebounding

*(13)* The girl was scared of high places, so she (　　　) her father's hand. She held it tightly as they looked out the window from the top of the tower.

**1** harassed **2** breached **3** drained **4** gripped

*(14)* Akiko could not help but be (       ) when she saw her colleagues having a quiet conversation. She moved closer to them to hear what they were talking about.

**1** obedient       **2** flexible       **3** sinful       **4** nosy

*(15)* Due to the snowstorm, the climbers were unable to reach the mountain's (       ). They had to turn around just a few hundred meters from the top.

**1** subsidy       **2** mirage       **3** summit       **4** crutch

*(16)* When Jonathan started at his company, he was often (       ) all day. However, after a few months, he took on more tasks and now has little free time.

**1** idle       **2** agile       **3** sane       **4** needy

*(17)* *A:* Guess what? I've got an interview for that job as a TV announcer!
*B:* That's great, but don't be too (       ) just yet. There'll be a lot of competition for that position.

**1** courteous       **2** optimistic       **3** suspicious       **4** flustered

*(18)* During her commute, Josie found the noise from the earphones of the train passenger next to her so (       ) that she decided to move to another seat.

**1** bothersome       **2** compelling       **3** flattering       **4** daring

*(19)* *A:* I couldn't believe how crowded this year's summer parade was.
*B:* I know! There were so many (       ) in the streets I could barely move.

**1** patriots       **2** spectators       **3** mimics       **4** executives

*(20)* Joseph was not sure if he could afford a taxi home from work, but after checking his wallet, he found that he had (       ) money for the ride.

**1** ample       **2** regal       **3** vain       **4** crafty

*(21)* ( ) involvement has been shown to enhance student performance in school. One example is helping children with schoolwork at home.

**1** Obsolete **2** Numb **3** Parental **4** Infamous

*(22)* Over the past few decades, many species have nearly been ( ) by pollution. However, recent conservation efforts are helping some of them to recover.

**1** wiped out **2** broken up **3** fixed up **4** turned down

*(23)* Dave was happy when his neighbor gave him a basket of fresh vegetables, but when he got home, he realized he did not know how to ( ) cooking them.

**1** go about **2** pull out **3** take in **4** bring down

*(24)* **A:** Our company allows employees to wear comfortable clothes, as long as they don't look too unprofessional.

**B:** That's new for me. Wearing casual clothes was ( ) at my last job.

**1** frowned upon **2** carried on
**3** entered into **4** crossed off

*(25)* The regional manager visited the small branch office last week and ( ) a few meetings to observe how things were going there.

**1** went back on **2** sat in on
**3** spoke down to **4** looked up to

45

## 2

*Read each passage and choose the best word or phrase from among the four choices for each blank. Then, on your answer sheet, find the number of the question and mark your answer.*

# The Documentary Boom

In recent years, the growth of TV streaming services has created a huge new market for documentaries. The number of documentaries being made has skyrocketed, providing welcome new opportunities for filmmakers, but there are also negative aspects. One issue is that many filmmakers feel they are ( *26* ). Some documentaries have attracted huge audiences and brought tremendous financial returns, so companies that operate streaming services have become more generous with their production budgets. With so much money involved, the intense pressure often makes filmmakers feel as though they have no choice but to alter the stories they tell to give them greater commercial appeal.

This has led to concerns regarding the ( *27* ) documentaries. While documentaries used to be considered a form of investigative journalism, there has been a noticeable shift in their subject matter. As the popularity of genres such as true crime has increased, the line between factual information and entertainment has become blurred. Documentaries, which were once devoted to informing viewers and raising awareness of problems in society, are too frequently becoming sensationalist entertainment designed primarily to shock or excite viewers.

Another worrying trend for filmmakers is the rise of celebrity documentaries. In the past, filmmakers generally followed the journalistic tradition of not paying ordinary subjects of documentaries for fear that doing so would encourage people to exaggerate or tell outright lies. Famous people, such as musicians, however, are now paid millions of dollars for their stories—often because such stars are guaranteed to attract viewers. ( *28* ), noncelebrities are also starting to demand compensation, which is creating a moral dilemma for filmmakers.

*(26)* **1** still being ignored
**2** not being paid enough
**3** losing control over content
**4** in need of large budgets

*(27)* **1** way people interpret
**2** people who appear in
**3** growing costs of creating
**4** decreasing social value of

*(28)* **1** Above all
**2** Understandably
**3** In contrast
**4** Nevertheless

# Anting

The field of ethology involves studying animals in their natural habitats to understand their behavior. Drawing conclusions about the reasons behind what animals do, however, is not always easy. Certain birds, for example, display a behavior called "anting." This usually involves a bird picking up some ants with its beak and rubbing them on its feathers. ( **29** ), birds have even been observed sitting on anthills with their wings spread out and allowing ants to crawl all over their bodies. Despite extensive observation, ethologists remain unsure why birds engage in this behavior.

One popular theory is that ( **30** ). Ants naturally produce a substance called formic acid that protects them against bacteria and fungi, and which is also toxic to other insects. If this substance is rubbed onto a bird's feathers, it could help inhibit disease and deter harmful pests. While birds commonly use ants, some have been seen picking up certain beetles and millipedes instead. The fact that these organisms also produce chemicals that keep harmful pests away provides support for this theory.

Another proposed idea is that rubbing ants on a bird's feathers ( **31** ). In an experiment, scientists discovered that some birds were more likely to consume ants that had their formic acid removed by the scientists than ants that retained the chemical. The formic acid is stored in a sac located next to an ant's nutrient-rich abdomen. Anting, some scientists suspect, may cause ants to release their formic acid without birds having to try to remove the sacs with their beaks—a process that could damage the area of ants that makes them such an appealing snack.

*(29)*  **1**  In other words
    **2**  For one thing
    **3**  Similarly
    **4**  Consequently

*(30)*  **1**  the ants eat organisms that harm the birds
    **2**  the behavior contributes to birds' health
    **3**  the behavior helps control ant populations
    **4**  the birds are trying to attract other insects

*(31)*  **1**  helps remove damaged feathers
    **2**  transfers nutrients to the ants
    **3**  increases the bird's appetite
    **4**  prepares the ants to be eaten

*Read each passage and choose the best answer from among the four choices for each question. Then, on your answer sheet, find the number of the question and mark your answer.*

# The Development of Colleges in the United States

Selling land is a common way to increase wealth, but for rural landowners in the United States during the nineteenth century, this was not always easy. Rural populations at the time were small, so landowners needed ways to attract buyers. One method was to keep prices low, but landowners also turned to another strategy: building colleges. Doing this made the land in their area more desirable, as colleges were centers of culture and learning. Colleges were built at an incredibly rapid pace, and by 1880, there were five times more colleges in the United States than there were in Europe.

With the exception of a few older, elite institutions, most US colleges only had a small number of students and instructors. Rather than being scholars, the faculty members were often religious men representing the different branches of Christianity that existed in the United States at the time. Administrators knew this would help to attract students from those religious organizations. Gaining admission to colleges was generally not difficult as long as students could pay the tuition, which, as a result of fierce competition to recruit students, was kept low. Unfortunately, low student numbers meant that many colleges were forced to close down, and those that survived could only continue operating through constant fundraising.

Demand for higher education, however, continued to increase along with the US population in the twentieth century. As the remaining colleges had well-established infrastructures, including land, buildings, and libraries, they were in a good position to accommodate this demand. Furthermore, they generally offered high-quality education and good sports and leisure facilities because one way they had survived was by being sensitive to students' needs. Another way the colleges ensured their futures was by maintaining close ties with their graduates, from whom they would receive generous donations. All of these factors have helped the US college system to transform itself into one of the most successful in the world.

(32) Why were so many colleges built in the United States in the nineteenth century?
**1** Increasing levels of wealth in rural areas led to more families wanting their children to receive a college education.
**2** Wealthy landowners built colleges as a way to improve their public image and ensure that they would be remembered after their death.
**3** Europeans living in the United States wanted colleges that would provide the same level of education that was available in their home countries.
**4** Building colleges was a way for people who owned land in rural areas to increase the value of their land and attract more buyers.

(33) What is true regarding many faculty members at US colleges in the nineteenth century?
**1** They quit after a short time because of the poor conditions they were forced to work under.
**2** Their salaries were usually paid by religious organizations rather than by the colleges themselves.
**3** There was a high degree of competition among them to gain the best positions at the colleges.
**4** Their religious backgrounds tended to be an effective way to get students to enroll at their colleges.

(34) One reason US colleges succeeded in the twentieth century was that they
**1** formed partnerships with local sports teams to increase the quality of their physical education programs.
**2** were able to increase their financial security by creating lasting relationships with their former students.
**3** decreased the competition with other colleges by focusing on recruiting students mostly from their local areas.
**4** kept their costs down by using facilities already available in the community instead of building their own.

# Machine or Human?

In 2004, NASA's exploration rover Opportunity landed on Mars. The golf-cart-sized rover, which was nicknamed "Oppy," was sent to survey the planet and capture images of its surface. Oppy's mission was supposed to last 90 days, but the rover continued to beam pictures and data back to Earth for the next 15 years. During that time, it captured the public's imagination. In fact, people became so attached to Oppy that when it ceased to function, they sent messages of condolence over social media similar to those intended for a deceased person.

The act of giving human traits to nonhuman things, which is known as anthropomorphism, is something humans do naturally, even at a young age. It is not unusual, for example, for people of all ages to form emotional attachments to objects such as toys, cars, and homes. Even the engineers, who frequently referred to Oppy as "she" or thought of it as a child, were not immune to this tendency. One effect of projecting human qualities onto a nonliving object seems to be that this makes people feel protective of it and brings out concern for its well-being. NASA appears to have utilized this phenomenon to its advantage by deliberately making Oppy seem more human, designing it with eyelike camera lenses in a headlike structure that extended from its body. Prior to the Opportunity mission, well-publicized failures had weakened public confidence in NASA, and the agency's funding had been reduced. It has been suggested that giving Oppy human characteristics was an effective strategy to win over the public and perhaps even attract additional funding for NASA's mission.

While thinking of Oppy as a human may seem harmless, there can be unfortunate consequences to anthropomorphizing objects. Assuming AI works in the same way as the human brain, for example, may lead to unrealistic expectations of its capabilities, causing it to be used in situations where it is unable to provide significant benefits. Anthropomorphism can also make people apprehensive of nightmare scenarios, such as AI and machines rising up in rebellion against humans. This idea of machines as a threat arises from the misunderstanding that they reason in the same way as humans do. It appears, however, that people cannot help themselves from anthropomorphizing. As journalist

Scott Simon writes, "if you spend a lot of time with a mechanism—talk to it, wait to hear from it and worry about it—even scientists begin to see personality in machinery."

(35) What do we learn about people's reactions to Oppy?
1  People immediately supported Oppy because they were interested in any new discoveries about Mars.
2  People found it difficult to relate to Oppy because little effort had been made to inform them about the significance of its mission.
3  People soon lost interest in Oppy's mission because the information Oppy sent back to Earth was too technical for nonscientists to understand.
4  People felt such an emotional connection to Oppy that they expressed sympathy for it when it stopped operating.

(36) According to the second paragraph, it seems likely that making Oppy appear more human was
1  a strategy designed to increase overall support for NASA's activities and to help it receive more money.
2  based on experiments in which children showed an increased interest in robots that looked like humans.
3  done because psychologists suggested that the strategy would make the engineers work harder to complete it on time.
4  the result of government pressure on NASA to make its designs more likely to be used in toys.

(37) According to the passage, what is a potential problem with anthropomorphism?
1  It can make people rely on machines to perform tasks that would be cheaper for humans to do themselves.
2  It can make people mistakenly assume that AI and machines do not need any guidance to perform tasks correctly.
3  The belief that AI and machines act in a similar way to humans can cause people to misunderstand what they are able to do.
4  The relationships scientists form with AI can cause them to prioritize its development over the needs of humans.

# The Marian Reforms

Around the end of the second century BC, the Roman Republic faced the threat of an invasion by tribal peoples from Western Europe and experienced a series of humiliating defeats in Africa. Realizing that the Roman army was no longer able to meet the needs of the rapidly expanding republic, the Roman leader Gaius Marius set about implementing sweeping reforms. These became known as the Marian reforms, and they transformed the Roman army into a nearly unstoppable military machine that was arguably the most effective fighting force in ancient times. Traditionally, enlistment of soldiers into the Roman army had been on a temporary basis, which necessitated constant recruitment and inevitably led to new recruits often having no previous fighting experience. Furthermore, property ownership was required for entry into the army, and increasing poverty within the Roman Republic severely reduced the pool of potential recruits who could meet this requirement.

The Marian reforms consisted of several measures, including the removal of both property requirements and the need for recruits to prepare their own weapons and armor. This allowed even the poorest citizens to enlist and led to better-equipped soldiers because the army could standardize and improve the weapons and armor used. Soldiers in the army became known as "legionaries," and they were trained in military strategy. Perhaps most importantly, the reforms provided a crucial incentive for enlistment—any soldier who served for 16 years was compensated with a plot of farmland and full Roman citizenship. The rapid expansion of the Roman Republic meant there were many noncitizen inhabitants who lived in poverty and for whom an opportunity to escape their situation was hugely appealing.

The Roman army's better-trained and more highly motivated soldiers led to it achieving significant military triumphs that contributed to Rome's expansion. The land that former legionaries received was generally in newly conquered provinces, so these veterans were instrumental in spreading Roman culture. Their presence also made it easier to overcome local resistance to Roman rule and facilitated the process of integration into the Roman Republic. The mere presence of the veterans brought greater security to new territories, since they could assist in preventing rebellions and resisting invasions.

While the Marian reforms greatly improved the Roman army, they also had an unexpected impact on Roman society that eventually led to the downfall of the republic. When the army was composed mostly of wealthy citizens enlisted on an as-needed basis, it had little influence on Roman politics. Following the Marian reforms, however, legionaries in the army became highly disciplined and developed an intense loyalty to their generals. In consequence, generals found it difficult to resist the temptation to use the forces under their command to gain political influence for themselves rather than to ensure the protection and expansion of the Roman Republic. This resulted in civil wars, and eventually, Julius Caesar successfully used the army to overthrow the elected government and declare himself the Roman leader. This marked the end of the relatively democratic Roman Republic and paved the way for the creation of a dictatorship ruled by all-powerful emperors.

*(38)* What was one reason for the Marian reforms?

**1** Financial problems within the Roman Republic meant a Roman leader had no choice but to reduce funding for the military.

**2** As the number of soldiers in the army increased, it became more difficult to transport them to Western Europe and Africa to defend the Roman Republic.

**3** Complaints arose among soldiers because they were forced to stay in the army for many years and received low pay for their service.

**4** A Roman leader was concerned that the army did not have the manpower or skills required to allow the Roman Republic to achieve its military goals.

*(39)* What was an important change that occurred because of the Marian reforms?

**1** A rule was introduced stating that only Roman citizens could join the Roman army, leading to more people trying to get Roman citizenship.

**2** Serving in the Roman army became more attractive because it was a way for people living in the Roman Republic to improve their lives.

**3** The Roman army struggled to find enough recruits because it would only accept men who already had military experience.

**4** The number of years that soldiers were required to spend in the Roman army was reduced, which lowered the average age of soldiers.

*(40)* According to the third paragraph, after the Roman army took over new territories,

**1** the number of soldiers sent to those areas would be greatly increased to allow the army to attack neighboring regions and continue the expansion of the Roman Republic.

**2** local people were invited to Rome's capital to learn the Roman language and culture so that they could quickly become accustomed to Roman society.

**3** ex-soldiers were given land there, which made it much easier to control the local people and ensure that the areas could be defended from various threats.

**4** the areas were often lost again quite quickly because it was impossible for the army to prevent the many rebellions that occurred.

*(41)* What effect did the Marian reforms have on Roman society?

**1** The army was used as a political tool, creating a system in which a Roman leader gained his position by military power rather than by being chosen by the people.

**2** The wealth and social standing of people who refused to serve in the army decreased, while former legionaries often obtained high government positions.

**3** The Roman army became so large that the cost of maintaining it became a major cause of the fall of the Roman Republic.

**4** The lack of discipline among the legionaries led to tension between Roman citizens and the army, which eventually resulted in civil wars.

**4**

● Write an essay on the given TOPIC.
● Use TWO of the POINTS below to support your answer.
● Structure: introduction, main body, and conclusion
● Suggested length: 120-150 words
● Write your essay in the space provided on Side B of your answer sheet. Any writing outside the space will not be graded.

## TOPIC

*Should companies be required to produce goods that are easy to recycle?*

## POINTS

● *Company profits*
● *Customer demand*
● *Pollution*
● *Product quality*

# ●一次試験 · **Listening Test**

**There are three parts to this listening test.**

| Part 1 | **Dialogues:** | 1 question each | Multiple-choice |
| Part 2 | **Passages:** | 2 questions each | Multiple-choice |
| Part 3 | **Real-Life:** | 1 question each | Multiple-choice |

※ Listen carefully to the instructions.

## Part 1

**No. 1**

1 He cannot find his e-reader.
2 He does not want to buy e-books.
3 He has broken his e-reader.
4 He finds it hard to download e-books.

**No. 2**

1 Take private yoga classes.
2 Find a different activity.
3 Continue with his current class.
4 Join another yoga group.

**No. 3**

1 She has some new ideas for the division.
2 She knows little about publishing.
3 She was an excellent student.
4 She wants to increase staff salaries.

**No. 4**

1 She wants to help a family in need.
2 They no longer fit her well.
3 There is an event at her school.
4 She does not have storage space for them.

**No. 5**

1 It will help reduce his workload.
2 It will mean more work with independent agents.
3 It will make his company more successful.
4 It will lead to many staff being fired.

**No. 6**

1 They will become less expensive in the future.
2 They would not save the couple money.
3 They need to be replaced after a few years.
4 They do not have many environmental benefits.

**No. 7**

CD 青-8

**1** Miki has not completed her translation work.
**2** The deadline is likely to change.
**3** The client has made a number of mistakes.
**4** Miki often does not work carefully enough.

**No. 8**

CD 青-9

**1** He found many online complaints.
**2** The cost of the cruise has increased.
**3** He cannot get time off from work.
**4** He is unable to book another cruise.

**No. 9**

CD 青-10

**1** It has a lot of unique characters.
**2** The show's writing has improved greatly.
**3** The plot was hard to predict.
**4** It may not be renewed for another season.

**No. 10**

CD 青-11

**1** He is busier than Yasuhiro.
**2** He does not get along with Genevieve.
**3** He often makes poor decisions.
**4** He may not have enough experience.

**No. 11**

CD 青-12

**1** Her lectures tend to be long.
**2** She gives too much homework.
**3** Her political views are extreme.
**4** She does not grade fairly.

**No. 12**

CD 青-13

**1** Search for solutions online.
**2** Get help from a professional.
**3** Ask their neighbors for advice.
**4** Move to a quieter neighborhood.

CD 青

## Part 2

*(A)*

**No. 13**

1 To improve the quality of their crops.
2 To give thanks for the food they grew.
3 To pray they could leave the desert.
4 To celebrate their time in Egypt.

**No. 14**

1 They have desert images on the walls.
2 They are covered to keep them cool.
3 Meals must be cooked in them.
4 People can see the sky from inside them.

*(B)*

**No. 15**

1 Vultures help stop them from affecting humans.
2 Vultures often spread them to other animals.
3 They can be deadly to vultures.
4 They survive in vultures' stomachs.

**No. 16**

1 Vultures' feeding habits help to reduce its effects.
2 It has increased vulture populations worldwide.
3 Vultures' food sources have changed because of it.
4 It has forced vultures to find new habitats.

*(C)*

**No. 17**

1 Workers often think they do not deserve praise.
2 Random praise can improve performance.
3 Too much praise can hurt performance.
4 Most bosses do not give enough praise.

**No. 18**

1 They tend to react negatively to praise.
2 They worry too much about their work.
3 They may benefit from having a growth mindset.
4 They affect the mindsets of workers around them.

*(D)*

**No. 19**
1 They believed an invasion would not happen.
2 They worried that the art would be destroyed.
3 They thought Canada was likely to be invaded.
4 They feared Germans would be able to steal the art.

**No. 20**
1 The importance of art during wartime.
2 A way to create larger mines.
3 The effects of low temperatures on paintings.
4 Ways of keeping art in good condition.

*(E)*

**No. 21**
1 To help warn about an attack.
2 To check the location of British soldiers.
3 To gather supplies for American troops.
4 To lead her father away from danger.

**No. 22**
1 There is evidence a different woman rode that night.
2 There are no records of an attack by the British army.
3 It was not officially documented.
4 A history book claims it did not happen.

*(F)*

**No. 23**
1 They had to relocate to more-populated areas.
2 They had to close due to unhappy customers.
3 They were not receiving enough snow.
4 They were opposed to using artificial snow.

**No. 24**
1 The use of artificial snow has hurt its business.
2 It makes use of the wind to help it operate.
3 It provides snow to other ski resorts in its local area.
4 Its slopes are at unusually high altitudes.

## Part 3

*(G)*

**No. 25**

***Situation:*** You are staying at a hotel. It is 6:30 p.m. now, and you want to have dinner at a nearby restaurant around 7:00 p.m. The concierge tells you the following.

***Question:*** Which restaurant should you choose?

**1**  Kingsley's.
**2**  Shrimp Lover.
**3**  Randy's.
**4**  Boca.

*(H)*

**No. 26**

***Situation:*** You have decided to sell half of your collection of 500 music CDs. You call a shop that buys and sells used CDs and hear the following recorded message.

***Question:*** What should you do?

**1**  Start the sales procedure online.
**2**  Begin packing your CDs into boxes.
**3**  Download a form from the website.
**4**  Make an appointment for an assessment.

*(I)*
**No. 27**

*Situation:* You are a college student. You want to learn about ancient Greeks and Romans and do not like group work. You are listening to an academic adviser's explanation.

*Question:* Which class should you take?

**1** History 103.
**2** Philosophy 105.
**3** History 202.
**4** Latin 102.

*(J)*
**No. 28**

*Situation:* The tablet computer you bought for your daughter two weeks ago has broken. It has a one-year warranty. You call the product manufacturer and hear the following recorded message.

*Question:* What should you do?

**1** Press 1.
**2** Press 2.
**3** Press 3.
**4** Press 4.

*(K)*
**No. 29**

*Situation:* You and your seven-year-old son are at a science museum. You want to take a tour. You must leave the museum in 45 minutes. You hear the following announcement.

*Question:* Which tour should you choose?

**1** Spark of Genius.
**2** The Age of Dinos.
**3** Deep into the Sea.
**4** Museum after Dark.

# ●二次試験・面接

※本書では出題例として2種類のカードを掲載していますが，本番では1枚のみ渡されます。
※面接委員の質問など，二次試験に関する音声はCDに収録されていません。

## 受験者用問題　カード　A

You have **one minute** to prepare.

This is a story about a couple who liked traveling.
You have **two minutes** to narrate the story.

Your story should begin with the following sentence:
**One day, a couple was talking at a café.**

No.1    Please look at the fourth picture. If you were the woman, what would you be thinking?

Now, Mr. / Ms. _____, please turn over the card and put it down.

No.2    Will Japan continue to be a popular tourist destination in the future?

No.3    Do you think employees in the service industry are treated well enough by their employers?

No.4    Is people's quality of life these days better than it was in the past?

You have **one minute** to prepare.

This is a story about a couple whose son liked sports.
You have **two minutes** to narrate the story.

Your story should begin with the following sentence:
**One day, a family was at home.**

No.1      Please look at the fourth picture.  If you were the father, what would you be thinking?

Now, Mr. / Ms. _____, please turn over the card and put it down.

No.2      Should playing video games be considered a sport?

No.3      Do you think parents should discuss important family issues with their children?

No.4      Should the government provide more university scholarships for students?

# 準1級

## 2023年度 第❶回

**一次試験** 2023.6.4実施

**二次試験** A日程 2023.7.2実施
B日程 2023.7.9実施
C日程 2023.7.16実施

**一次試験・筆記(90分)**
pp.70〜85

**一次試験・リスニング(約32分)**
pp.86〜91
CD青-27〜52

**二次試験・面接(約8分)**
pp.92〜95

※解答一覧は別冊p.47
※解答と解説は別冊pp.48〜90

※別冊の巻末についている解答用マークシートを使いましょう。

## 合格基準スコア

●**一次試験**……1792
(満点2250/リーディング750, リスニング750, ライティング750)
●**二次試験**……512(満点750/スピーキング750)

# ●一次試験・筆記

**1** To complete each item, choose the best word or phrase from among the four choices. Then, on your answer sheet, find the number of the question and mark your answer.

*(1)* At first, Mick was (          ) by the idea of going to live abroad by himself.  Once he did it, however, it was less difficult than he had feared.
**1** pacified　　**2** restored　　**3** daunted　　**4** tackled

*(2)* Students are advised to pace their studying throughout the semester instead of (          ) right before their exams.
**1** cramming　　**2** detaining　　**3** swelling　　**4** embracing

*(3)* The two candidates' tempers (          ) during the presidential debate. They angrily attacked each other's positions on issues throughout the night.
**1** flared　　**2** digested　　**3** professed　　**4** tumbled

*(4)* Many banks required government (          ) to stay in business after the stock market crash.  The help mostly came in the form of large loans.
**1** intervention　　　　　　**2** appreciation
**3** accumulation　　　　　　**4** starvation

*(5)* Police must follow strict (          ) at a crime scene to make sure the evidence is not damaged or altered in any way.
**1** tributes　　**2** protocols　　**3** reservoirs　　**4** portions

*(6)* The umpire (          ) the two players for fighting.  They were not allowed to play in the rest of the game.
**1** slaughtered　　　　　　**2** administered
**3** ejected　　　　　　　　**4** conceived

*(7)* | Cats are known to be protective of their (　　　). They often attack other animals that they think could be a threat to their kittens.
**1** prey **2** offspring **3** rituals **4** remains

*(8)* | Fans of Greenville United were disappointed when the team's poor performance throughout the season led to its (　　　) from the A-League to the B-League.
**1** demotion **2** craving **3** aggravation **4** hassle

*(9)* | Bibi loves hiking and playing sports, so she needs clothes that do not wear out too quickly. When she goes shopping, she generally buys clothing that is (　　　).
**1** swift **2** aloof **3** shallow **4** durable

*(10)* | Consumers should not (　　　) any personal information to callers claiming to be from the bank, as such calls are sometimes from criminals.
**1** sway **2** detest
**3** contemplate **4** disclose

*(11)* | Because the tennis champion is unfriendly to other players and claims he is the greatest player who has ever lived, he is often criticized for his (　　　).
**1** commodity **2** arrogance **3** neutrality **4** specimen

*(12)* | Many readers found the author's novels (　　　). He was known for writing long, confusing sentences that had no clear meaning.
**1** genuine **2** impending
**3** subdued **4** incomprehensible

*(13)* | "Class, I want you all to listen very (　　　)," the teacher said. "Much of what I will say is not in the textbook but will be on the test."
**1** attentively **2** consecutively
**3** wearily **4** eloquently

*(14)* The school is known for being at the ( ) of education. Its teachers use the newest teaching methods and the latest technology in the classroom.

**1** forefront    **2** lapse    **3** doctrine    **4** myth

*(15)* The mayor used ( ) language in his speech because he thought it was extremely important that the citizens support his plan for public transportation.

**1** forceful    **2** merciful    **3** futile    **4** tranquil

*(16)* When the pop singer died, she left her favorite charity a ( ) of over $10 million. "We are so grateful for her generosity," said a charity spokesperson.

**1** rhyme    **2** justice    **3** legacy    **4** majority

*(17)* As they approached the top of the mountain, some of the hikers began to feel sick because of the low oxygen levels at the high ( ).

**1** apparatus    **2** equation    **3** altitude    **4** mileage

*(18)* Ted lives on a ( ) income. He makes just enough to afford a small apartment, pay his bills, and occasionally go out for dinner.

**1** blissful    **2** modest    **3** showy    **4** sturdy

*(19)* The carpenter was careful to choose a ( ) piece of wood for the table. There would be problems if it did not have the same thickness throughout.

**1** reckless    **2** gaping    **3** dreary    **4** uniform

*(20)* Although Pieter was a private, quiet man who rarely showed his ( ) for his children, they knew that he truly loved them.

**1** affection    **2** circulation   **3** oppression   **4** coalition

(21) Anton heard a strange (　　　) coming from his speakers, so he checked to make sure all the cables were properly connected.

**1** buzz　　　　**2** peck　　　　**3** thorn　　　　**4** core

(22) Late last night, a man was caught trying to (　　　) a convenience store. The police forced him to drop his weapon and arrested him.

**1** shrug off　　**2** sit out　　　**3** run against　**4** hold up

(23) Jill had always loved France, so when there was a chance to work in her company's Paris office, she (　　　) it. In fact, she was the first to apply.

**1** plowed through　　　　　　**2** pulled on
**3** threw off　　　　　　　　**4** jumped at

(24) *A:* How's the class you signed up for going to (　　　) with your work schedule?
*B:* It's online, and I can study at my own pace. I can read the material when I get home from work, so it should be fine.

**1** get over　　　**2** fit in　　　**3** hold onto　　**4** take after

(25) Before moving to her new section, Betty will (　　　) all of her current projects to the person who will be doing her job from now on.

**1** beef up　　　**2** bank on　　　**3** hand over　　**4** slip by

Read each passage and choose the best word or phrase from among the four choices for each blank. Then, on your answer sheet, find the number of the question and mark your answer.

# Beyond Small Talk

Research indicates that the relationships people have can influence their well-being. Positive relationships not only lead to increased happiness but also have a beneficial effect on physical health. So far, most studies have focused on relationships with people we are close to, such as family members or friends. This makes sense, as when we have a problem or want to share our thoughts and opinions, we are most likely to talk to such people. ( *26* ), some recent studies have explored how we interact with strangers, and the results were rather surprising.

In one study, subjects were paired up with someone they had never met before, and each pair was asked to come up with a light discussion topic, such as the weather, and a more substantial one, such as their personal goals. At the beginning of the study, most subjects thought they would enjoy casual conversations more. After each conversation, the subjects were asked to rate it based on enjoyment and feeling of connection with their partners. The results showed that the ( *27* ). That is, most subjects reported having a more positive experience overall after discussing serious topics.

The study's results suggest that people would benefit from interacting on a deeper level with strangers. In fact, the subjects in the study generally expressed a desire to have meaningful conversations with people they did not know more often in their lives. However, they also thought that ( *28* ). The researchers believe that this assumption is incorrect, and that, for the most part, strangers are also interested in going beyond casual conversation.

(26) **1** In exchange
**2** For instance
**3** In contrast
**4** In short

(27) **1** topics had made the subjects nervous
**2** subjects' ratings did not always match
**3** topic choices had been too varied
**4** subjects' expectations had been wrong

(28) **1** communicating clearly would be difficult
**2** other people did not share this desire
**3** their family members would not approve
**4** their privacy should come first

# The Thing

After spending nearly a decade on a museum shelf in Chile, a mysterious fossil known as "The Thing" has finally been identified. Researchers now believe it is a 66-million-year-old soft-shelled egg and that it probably contained a mosasaur, a large aquatic reptile that existed around the same time as dinosaurs. Previous fossil evidence had suggested that mosasaurs ( *29* ). The researchers' findings challenge this idea, however, and the researchers say the fossil's size and the fact that it was discovered in an area where mosasaur fossils have been found support their conclusion.

Although the researchers are excited to have identified The Thing, it has opened a new debate. One theory suggests mosasaurs would have laid their eggs in open water, with the young hatching almost immediately. ( *30* ), some scientists believe the mosasaurs would have laid their eggs on the beach and buried them, much like some modern reptiles do. Further research, it is hoped, will reveal which of these is correct.

Another group of researchers from the United States has shed additional light on the eggs of prehistoric creatures after taking a closer look at previously discovered fossils of baby dinosaurs. It was believed that dinosaurs produced hard-shelled eggs, but the fossils on which this assumption was based represent a limited number of dinosaur species. Through their analysis, the US researchers discovered evidence that suggests the eggs of early dinosaurs were, in fact, soft-shelled. If true, this could explain why ( *31* ). Since softer materials break down easily, they are much less likely to be preserved in the fossil record.

*(29)* **1** were likely hunted by dinosaurs
**2** relied on eggs for food
**3** did not lay eggs
**4** may not have existed with dinosaurs

*(30)* **1** Likewise
**2** On the other hand
**3** As a result
**4** For example

*(31)* **1** few dinosaur eggs have been found
**2** there are not more dinosaur species
**3** some dinosaurs were unable to produce eggs
**4** dinosaur babies often did not survive

# The Chicken of Tomorrow

Before the 1940s, most chickens in the United States were raised on family farms, and the main emphasis was on egg production rather than obtaining meat. Poverty and food shortages were common at that time, so people wanted to maintain a regular source of protein without sacrificing their chickens. Additionally, there were a tremendous variety of chickens being raised, as farmers generally chose a breed based on how well it was adapted to the local conditions—whether it was suited to a dry or a humid climate, for example.

After World War II, however, the growing availability of meat such as pork and beef meant eggs could not compete as a source of protein. The US Department of Agriculture therefore set up an event called the Chicken of Tomorrow contest to find a type of chicken that could be raised economically and produced more meat. The overall winner, which was a combination of different breeds, grew faster and larger than other types, and it could adapt to various climates. Inspired by the contest, breeding companies began creating complicated mixtures of chicken varieties to guarantee a consistent supply of birds with these same desirable features. Since producing such genetic combinations was difficult, most farmers had no choice but to purchase young chickens from those companies rather than breeding them by themselves—a development that completely changed the industry.

The contest helped popularize the consumption of chicken meat, but this trend also had a dark side. It became more economical to raise massive numbers of chickens in large facilities where they were confined in small cages. Not only did this force numerous small farms out of business, but it also created conditions for the birds that, according to animal rights activists, caused the chickens stress and led to higher levels of sickness. While the contest made chicken a regular food item, some people questioned whether it was worth it.

*(32)* What is one thing that we learn about the US chicken industry before the 1940s?

**1** The type of chicken raised on each farm usually depended on the climate in the area where the farm was located.

**2** Each farm would raise more than one type of chicken in case there was a sudden change in environmental conditions.

**3** Chickens were generally only eaten by very poor people or at times when there were food shortages.

**4** Because there were so many chicken farms across the country, many of the eggs produced ended up being wasted.

*(33)* The US Department of Agriculture organized the Chicken of Tomorrow contest because

**1** other types of meat, such as pork and beef, were becoming more expensive, so the American people wanted a cheaper alternative.

**2** most chicken farms were focused on egg production, which led to a need to create a chicken that was more suitable for producing meat.

**3** a large number of chicken farms in America went out of business, which severely decreased the availability of chicken meat.

**4** the American people were tired of eating the same type of eggs for so long, so producers wanted a different type of chicken.

*(34)* What is one way that the contest affected the chicken industry?

**1** Farmers learned that it was relatively easy to combine several types of chickens, which encouraged them to breed new varieties.

**2** Although the number of small chicken farms increased across America, many of these were often poorly run and had cheap facilities.

**3** It started a move toward keeping chickens in conditions that increased the birds' suffering and made them less healthy.

**4** Farmers realized that improving their farming methods could help them to raise chickens that produced more and better-tasting meat.

# *Discipline in American Schools*

For decades, methods of discipline used in American schools have been based on the theories of psychologist B. F. Skinner, who believed that systems of reward and punishment were the most effective methods of improving people's behavior. Commonly, students who break rules are given punishments, such as being prohibited from attending classes for a day or more or being made to stay in class after the school day ends. These are designed to teach the students to follow teachers' instructions and respect classmates. Recent psychological studies, however, have determined that as effective as punishment may be in bringing peace to the classroom temporarily, it can intensify the very behavior it is intended to correct when used continually over an extended period of time.

Many experts now believe that in order for children to learn to behave appropriately, it is essential that they develop self-control. When students are punished to make them obey the rules, they are being forced to adopt good behavior through external pressure. Self-control, on the other hand, comes from internal motivation, self-confidence, and the ability to be tolerant of others, and using punishment as a substitute for these things can actually delay or prevent their development. Similarly, the use of rewards such as stickers leads to students merely attempting to please the teacher rather than understanding the importance of gaining knowledge and social skills that will help them throughout their lives.

In recent years, an increasing amount of research has been backing up these ideas. A region of the brain known as the prefrontal cortex helps us to concentrate on tasks and is responsible for self-discipline and allowing us to consider the consequences of our actions. Research suggests that the prefrontal cortex may be less developed in students with behavioral problems. Fortunately, though, there is evidence that repeated experiences can alter the brain's structure, which suggests that it is also possible to influence the development of the prefrontal cortex. Child-behavior expert Ross Greene believes that when educators change their attitudes so that they actually listen to students' feelings about their bad behavior and encourage them to come up with solutions to the issues they face, this can have a physical effect on the prefrontal cortex. Greene has designed a highly successful program that has greatly reduced behavioral problems at many schools, and as a result of the extensive media coverage his ideas have received in recent years, they are being adopted by more and more educators.

(35) What has psychological research shown about the use of punishment in schools?
**1** It is only likely to be effective when it is used together with rewards in order to reduce its negative effects.
**2** Though it may succeed in producing better behavior in the short term, it can actually be harmful in the long term.
**3** There are various new types of punishment that are far more effective than physical punishment.
**4** Using some form of punishment is necessary for forcing students to obey teachers and respect their classmates.

(36) According to the passage, what is one effect the use of rewards has on students?
**1** It can teach them the advantages of hard work and make them better at focusing on their academic goals.
**2** It causes them to want material things and makes them less aware of the need to behave in ways that are pleasing to other people.
**3** It can prevent them from developing important skills that would be beneficial to them later in life.
**4** It helps them to realize the importance of deciding their own goals rather than just doing what their teachers tell them to do.

(37) What does Ross Greene believe about children's brains?
**1** Helping children solve their own problems can promote the development of the part of the brain that controls behavior.
**2** Since the brains of younger children function in a different way to those of older children, different methods of dealing with behavioral issues are necessary.
**3** The region of the brain known as the prefrontal cortex may be less important in controlling children's behavior than some scientists believe it is.
**4** Bad behavior does not only have a negative effect on children's academic performance but also permanently prevents the normal development of their brains.

# Robert the Bruce and the Declaration of Arbroath

In 1286, the sudden death of King Alexander III of Scotland resulted in a power struggle among various nobles that nearly brought the country to civil war. To settle the matter, England's King Edward I was asked to select a new ruler from among the rivals. Edward, who himself had ambitions to ultimately rule Scotland, agreed only on the condition that the new leader pledged loyalty to him. He chose a noble named John Balliol as the new king, but resentment soon grew as England repeatedly exerted its authority over Scotland's affairs. The turning point came when Edward attempted to force Scotland to provide military assistance in England's conflict with France. When Balliol allied his nation with France instead, Edward invaded Scotland, defeated Balliol, and took the throne.

This was the situation faced by the Scottish noble Robert the Bruce as he attempted to free Scotland from English rule. Robert, whose father had been one of Balliol's rivals for the throne, gained political dominance and led a rebellion that drove English forces from Scotland. Robert was crowned king of Scotland in 1306, and although he enjoyed tremendous support domestically, he had angered the Pope, the leader of the Roman Catholic Church. Not only had he ignored the church's requests that he make peace with England, but he had also taken the life of his closest rival to the throne in a place of worship before being crowned king.

Scotland's leadership knew that the country would remain internationally isolated and vulnerable without the church's recognition. International acceptance of Scotland's independence would be especially important if the country were to exist in the shadow of a mighty nation like England, which still failed to officially acknowledge Robert as Scotland's king despite having retreated. In 1320, Scotland's most powerful nobles therefore gathered to create a document known today as the Declaration of Arbroath. It proclaimed Scotland's independence and requested the Pope recognize Robert as the country's ruler. The response the nobles received later in the year, however, indicated that the declaration initially had not been effective. The Pope not only refused Scotland's request but also failed to confirm its self-proclaimed independence, although he did urge England to pursue a peaceful resolution in its dealings with the nation. A few years later, however, the declaration's influence contributed to the Pope recognizing Robert and his kingdom after a peace treaty finally freed Scotland from England's threat.

Today, the Declaration of Arbroath is one of the most celebrated documents in Scottish history. Some historians even argue it inspired the US Declaration of Independence, although proof of this is lacking. Scholars generally agree, however, that what makes the Declaration of Arbroath so historic is the assertion that the king may rule only with the approval of the Scottish people; specifically, the nobles used the document to boldly insist on their right to remove any ruler who betrayed them. In this sense, the document was a pioneering example of a contract between a country's ruler and its people, in which the ruler was responsible for ensuring the people could live in a free society.

*(38)* What happened following the death of King Alexander III of Scotland?

**1** Scotland was able to trick King Edward I into choosing John Balliol even though it was not in Edward's interest to do so.

**2** King Edward I began to question the loyalty of the Scottish nobles who had not supported John Balliol's attempt to become king.

**3** King Edward I attempted to use the situation to his advantage in order to increase his power over Scotland.

**4** Scotland felt so threatened by France's military power that diplomatic relations between the countries worsened.

**(39)** What problem did Robert the Bruce face after he became king of Scotland?

**1** Although he was a great military leader, his lack of political skills led him to negotiate a poor agreement with England.

**2** The disagreements he had with his rivals about religion caused many Scottish people to stop supporting him.

**3** The religious differences between Scotland and England made it likely that Scotland would be attacked again.

**4** Because of the things he had done to gain power, Scotland could not get the support it needed to be safe from England.

**(40)** In the year the Declaration of Arbroath was written,

**1** it became clear that the Pope considered it a priority to recognize Scotland's independence as a nation.

**2** the Pope attempted to encourage peace between England and Scotland despite not acknowledging either Robert or his country.

**3** the promise of peace between England and Scotland was endangered by Scotland's attempt to get help from the Pope.

**4** Scotland was able to achieve enough international recognition to get the Pope to admit that Robert was the country's true king.

**(41)** What is one common interpretation of the Declaration of Arbroath?

**1** It demonstrates that Robert was actually a much better leader than people had originally thought him to be.

**2** It brought a new way of looking at the duty that a country's ruler had to the people he or she was governing.

**3** It reveals that there was much more conflict between Scottish rulers and nobles at the time than scholars once believed.

**4** It suggested that a beneficial system of government was not possible with a king or queen ruling a country.

**4**
- Write an essay on the given TOPIC.
- Use TWO of the POINTS below to support your answer.
- Structure: introduction, main body, and conclusion
- Suggested length: 120-150 words
- Write your essay in the space provided on Side B of your answer sheet. _Any writing outside the space will not be graded._

## TOPIC
*Should businesses provide more online services?*

## POINTS
- *Convenience*
- *Cost*
- *Jobs*
- *The environment*

# ⦿一次試験 · **Listening Test**

> **There are three parts to this listening test.**

| | | | |
|---|---|---|---|
| **Part 1** | **Dialogues:** | 1 question each | Multiple-choice |
| **Part 2** | **Passages:** | 2 questions each | Multiple-choice |
| **Part 3** | **Real-Life:** | 1 question each | Multiple-choice |

※ Listen carefully to the instructions.

## Part 1

**No. 1**

CD
青-28

1 Visit her brother in the hospital.
2 Submit her assignment.
3 Ask her brother for help.
4 Choose a new assignment topic.

**No. 2**

CD
青-29

1 Too much money is spent on education.
2 The budget is likely to be decreased soon.
3 The government is wasting money.
4 The media is unfair to the government.

**No. 3**

CD
青-30

1 The man will become much busier.
2 The woman will need to attend more meetings.
3 The woman dislikes the people on the fourth floor.
4 The man did not want his new position.

**No. 4**

CD
青-31

1 To give her a massage.
2 To pick up some food.
3 To give her a gift certificate.
4 To do some housework.

**No. 5**

CD
青-32

1 Ask the shop to replace the printer.
2 Get the old printer fixed.
3 Try to get money back from the shop.
4 Visit the shop to check other models.

**No. 6**

CD
青-33

1 His client canceled the deal.
2 The contract needed to be revised.
3 The lawyer made a serious mistake.
4 He arrived late for an important meeting.

**No. 7**

1 His boss does not trust him.
2 He has very tight deadlines.
3 He lacks the skills required.
4 His boss is not well organized.

**No. 8**

1 Get a new sofa right away.
2 Buy a sofa online.
3 Look for a sofa on sale.
4 Repair their current sofa.

**No. 9**

1 Checking the weather news.
2 Taking a trip to their cabin this weekend.
3 Preparing emergency supplies.
4 Going out for ice cream.

**No. 10**

1 She lacks enthusiasm for her job.
2 She is going to be dismissed.
3 She is unpopular with the clients.
4 She needs to improve her computer skills.

**No. 11**

1 The man should try to sell them for a profit.
2 They should be hung in an art gallery.
3 The man should find out what they are worth.
4 They should be displayed properly.

**No. 12**

1 He forgot to fill the water bottles.
2 He did not tell her the water would be turned off.
3 He lost the notices about the water pipe inspection.
4 He damaged the water pipes.

## Part 2

*(A)*

**No. 13**
1 When each of the crops is planted is important.
2 They only grow in a small region of North America.
3 They have difficulty competing with weeds.
4 There needs to be space between the plants.

**No. 14**
1 Use more-modern growing techniques.
2 Find new plants that can be grown in the desert.
3 Teach others how to grow the Three Sisters.
4 Recover forgotten growing methods.

*(B)*

**No. 15**
1 They do not give enough thought to their children's safety.
2 They are often forced to set strict rules for their children.
3 They should spend more time with their children.
4 They are giving their children a variety of experiences.

**No. 16**
1 Set times when streets are closed to cars.
2 Remove parking lots from playgrounds.
3 Build new roads outside the center of cities.
4 Make cars safer by changing their design.

*(C)*

**No. 17**
1 They explain how the rain forest formed.
2 They show what early humans looked like.
3 They include creatures that have died out.
4 They were used in religious ceremonies.

**No. 18**
1 They do not need to be preserved.
2 They were probably made by Europeans.
3 They used to be much more detailed.
4 They are not thousands of years old.

*(D)*

No. 19
1 It was based on a popular movie.
2 It gave away many luxury items.
3 It had weekly comedy competitions.
4 It led many people to buy TV sets.

No. 20
1 Starting a charity to support Black performers.
2 Fighting racism in the TV industry.
3 The unique advertisements he produced.
4 His amazing dancing ability.

*(E)*

No. 21
1 It occurs more often when people are younger.
2 Previous research on it had involved mainly male subjects.
3 It became more common after the nineteenth century.
4 People often mistake it for other feelings.

No. 22
1 Exploring large public locations.
2 Viewing spaces that had exactly the same furniture.
3 Performing the same activity in different spaces.
4 Entering a space with a familiar layout.

*(F)*

No. 23
1 They traveled faster than other arrows.
2 They were effective against armor.
3 They were the longest type of arrow.
4 They were commonly made with steel.

No. 24
1 He forced men to practice using longbows.
2 He was an expert at shooting a longbow.
3 He was badly injured in a longbow attack.
4 He sold longbows to foreign armies.

## Part 3

*(G)*

**No. 25**

***Situation:*** You need a bag to use during your upcoming business trip. You will also go hiking using the bag on your days off. A shop employee tells you the following.

***Question:*** Which bag should you buy?

**1** The Western.
**2** The Dangerfield.
**3** The Spartan.
**4** The Winfield.

*(H)*

**No. 26**

***Situation:*** You need to park your car near the airport for 16 days. You want the best price but are worried about your car being damaged. A friend tells you about options.

***Question:*** Which parking lot should you use?

**1** SKM Budget Parking.
**2** The Vanier Plaza Hotel.
**3** Nelson Street Skypark.
**4** The Econolodge.

*(I)*

**No. 27**

*Situation:* Your air conditioner suddenly stopped working, and its blue light is flashing. You call customer support and hear the following recorded message.

*Question:* What should you do first?

**1** Remove the air conditioner filter.
**2** Open up the air conditioner panel.
**3** Disconnect the air conditioner.
**4** Arrange a service appointment.

*(J)*

**No. 28**

*Situation:* You want to order a back issue of a monthly science magazine. You are interested in genetics. You call the magazine publisher and are told the following.

*Question:* Which issue should you order?

**1** The July issue.
**2** The August issue.
**3** The October issue.
**4** The November issue.

*(K)*

**No. 29**

*Situation:* You bought five cans of Bentham Foods tuna fish at the supermarket on May 30. You hear the following announcement on TV. You have not eaten any of the tuna.

*Question:* What should you do?

**1** Take the cans to the store you bought them at.
**2** Call the Bentham Foods recall hotline.
**3** Arrange to have the cans picked up.
**4** Visit the Bentham Foods website for instructions.

# ●二次試験・面接

※本書では出題例として2種類のカードを掲載していますが，本番では1枚のみ渡されます。
※面接委員の質問など，二次試験に関する音声はCDに収録されていません。

## 受験者用問題　カード　A

You have **one minute** to prepare.

This is a story about a university student who lived with his family.
You have **two minutes** to narrate the story.

Your story should begin with the following sentence:
**One day, a university student was watching TV with his mother and grandfather.**

No. 1  Please look at the fourth picture. If you were the university student, what would you be thinking?

Now, Mr. / Ms. _____, please turn over the card and put it down.

No. 2  Do you think parents should be stricter with their children?

No. 3  Can people trust the news that they see on TV these days?

No. 4  Will more people choose to work past retirement age in the future?

You have **one minute** to prepare.

This is a story about a woman who worked at a dentist's office.
You have **two minutes** to narrate the story.

Your story should begin with the following sentence:
**One day, a woman was working at the reception desk of a dentist's office.**

No.1 Please look at the fourth picture. If you were the woman, what would you be thinking?

Now, Mr. / Ms. _____, please turn over the card and put it down.

No. 2 Do you think it is harder to raise children now than it was in the past?

No. 3 Do you think companies focus too much on making their products cheaper?

No. 4 Will the government be able to meet the needs of Japan's aging society?

# 準 1 級

## 2022年度 第 3 回

| 一次試験 | 2023.1.22実施 |
| --- | --- |
| 二次試験 | A日程 2023.2.19実施<br>B日程 2023.2.26実施<br>C日程 2023.3.5実施 |

一次試験・筆記(90分)
pp.98〜113

一次試験・リスニング(約31分)
pp.114〜119
CD赤-1〜26

二次試験・面接(約8分)
pp.120〜123

※解答一覧は別冊p.91
※解答と解説は別冊pp.92〜134

※別冊の巻末についている解答用マークシートを使いましょう。

## 合格基準スコア

● 一次試験……1792
(満点2250/リーディング750, リスニング750, ライティング750)
● 二次試験……512(満点750/スピーキング750)

**1** To complete each item, choose the best word or phrase from among the four choices. Then, on your answer sheet, find the number of the question and mark your answer.

*(1)* Fernando has been (       ) to the success of the company, so everyone is worried about what will happen after he quits next month.

**1** desperate            **2** philosophical
**3** inadequate          **4** instrumental

*(2)* Some people feel the film was (       ). Although it did not win any awards, there are those who believe it was a great work of art.

**1** overtaken    **2** overridden    **3** underfed    **4** underrated

*(3)* More than 50 million people (       ) during World War II. That is more deaths than in any other war in history.

**1** worshiped    **2** perished    **3** haunted    **4** jeered

*(4)* Walt's restaurant serves dishes that were traditionally eaten by poor people in the countryside. He says (       ) were skilled at creating delicious meals from cheap ingredients.

**1** correspondents       **2** janitors
**3** captives              **4** peasants

*(5)* The discovery of a serious (       ) in the design plans for the new building caused the construction to be delayed by several months.

**1** clog    **2** boom    **3** flaw    **4** dump

*(6)* When it came time to deliver her presentation, Rachel found herself (       ) with fear. She simply stood in front of everyone, unable to speak.

**1** trimmed    **2** teased    **3** paralyzed    **4** acquired

*(7)* Despite the fact that the two countries had once fought each other in a war, they now enjoy an (     ) relationship and are, in fact, allies.
**1** alleged　　**2** amicable　　**3** abusive　　**4** adhesive

*(8)* Tina's new goal is to get healthy. In addition to including more vegetables in her diet, she has decided to (     ) an exercise program into her daily routine.
**1** commemorate　　　　　**2** alienate
**3** liberate　　　　　　　**4** incorporate

*(9)* Some historians believe the (     ) of dogs occurred over 10,000 years ago. They have been kept as pets and used to work on farms ever since.
**1** elevation　　　　　　　**2** domestication
**3** deception　　　　　　　**4** verification

*(10)* Oscar is well-known for his friendly personality and good manners. Every morning, he (     ) greets everyone in the office as he walks toward his desk.
**1** scarcely　　**2** courteously　　**3** tediously　　**4** obnoxiously

*(11)* The plan for a new library was put on hold because of a lack of funds. A few years later, however, the plan was (     ), and construction work started.
**1** deprived　　**2** revived　　**3** obstructed　　**4** agitated

*(12)* Maggie's grandmother has recently become very (     ). She now needs help to walk and cannot climb stairs by herself.
**1** poetic　　**2** savage　　**3** frail　　**4** rash

*(13)* The novelist likes to work in (     ). She says she can only write well when she is in her country house, which is located in an area with no people around.
**1** solitude　　**2** corruption　　**3** excess　　**4** consent

*(14)* Archaeologists found many (          ), including pieces of jewelry and pottery, while digging at the ancient burial ground. These will be given to the local history museum.

**1** setbacks **2** artifacts **3** pledges **4** salutes

*(15)* With faster Internet connections and better computers, more information can be (          ) at high speed than ever before.

**1** transmitted **2** rejoiced **3** nauseated **4** offended

*(16)* Maria criticized her brother and called him (          ) after she learned that he had lost all of his money gambling.

**1** pathetic **2** analytical **3** dedicated **4** ceaseless

*(17)* The architect was famous for designing buildings in a (          ) style. He wanted his designs to reflect current social and cultural trends.

**1** preceding **2** simultaneous
**3** plentiful **4** contemporary

*(18)* A lack of media (          ) left the town uninformed about the chemical leak. The media only started reporting about the incident once the leak was out of control.

**1** enrollment **2** coverage **3** assortment **4** leverage

*(19)* After years of spending more money than taxes brought in, the government now has a (          ) of trillions of dollars.

**1** fatigue **2** petition **3** deficit **4** conspiracy

*(20)* The artist made a living by (          ) detailed figures out of stone. In order to cut such a hard substance, she used a number of special tools.

**1** carving **2** luring **3** soothing **4** ranking

*(21)* Ruth watched from the bench as her team ran up and down the court. Unfortunately, a shoulder injury had forced her to (       ) from the game.

**1** withdraw    **2** bypass    **3** upgrade    **4** overload

*(22)* Jocelyn could see the storm (       ) from the west. The skies began to darken, and the wind gradually grew stronger.

**1** rolling in                **2** adding up
**3** holding out             **4** passing down

*(23)* The company suffered from five years of decreasing sales until it finally (       ). It closed its doors forever last week.

**1** dialed up               **2** went under
**3** came along            **4** pulled through

*(24)* The print on the contract was so small that Gus needed a magnifying glass to (       ) the words.

**1** make out    **2** tune up    **3** draw up    **4** blow out

*(25)* The cat was (       ) her newborn kittens. She became nervous whenever anyone stepped too close to them.

**1** packing up            **2** looking into
**3** watching over      **4** showing up

*Read each passage and choose the best word or phrase from among the four choices for each blank. Then, on your answer sheet, find the number of the question and mark your answer.*

# California Chinatown

In the late nineteenth century, Chinese immigrants to the United States faced significant discrimination from White Americans when looking for employment and accommodation. ( **26** ), they tended to live in neighborhoods known as Chinatowns, where there were better opportunities to find jobs and housing. One of the largest Chinatowns was in the city of San Jose, California, but because it was destroyed in a fire in 1887, little has been known about the lives of its inhabitants.

It was long assumed that the food items supplied to San Jose's Chinatown originated in Hong Kong and China. Recently, however, archaeologists' analysis of fish bones at a former trash pit has provided evidence that ( **27** ). These particular bones stood out because they belonged to a species known as the giant snakehead. Since the fish is native not to China or Hong Kong but rather to Southeast Asian nations, archaeologists believe it was transported to Hong Kong after being caught elsewhere, then shipped to the United States for consumption.

While the discovery offers insight into the complexity of the trade networks that supplied San Jose's Chinatown, other discoveries at the site have revealed information about the lifestyles of the neighborhood's immigrant residents. For example, it seems residents ( **28** ). While the presence of cow remains suggests residents had adopted the Western habit of eating beef, pig bones were the most common type of animal remains archaeologists discovered. As pork was a staple of the diets in their home country, the bones indicate the custom of raising and consuming pigs continued among the immigrants.

*(26)*  **1**  Consequently
    **2**  Despite this
    **3**  Similarly
    **4**  In contrast

*(27)*  **1**  has led to more mystery
    **2**  many foods were of poor quality
    **3**  this was not always the case
    **4**  not all shipments arrived safely

*(28)*  **1**  were more divided than previously thought
    **2**  often sent packages to China
    **3**  struggled to obtain enough food
    **4**  maintained some of their food traditions

# Plant Plan

Most flowering plants rely on insects for pollination. When an insect makes contact with a flower, it gets pollen on its body. Then, when the insect moves around on the plant or visits another plant of the same species, this pollen comes into contact with the female part of that plant. This pollination process allows plant reproduction to occur. ( **29** ), the plants usually provide something the insect needs, such as a meal of nectar.

Flowering plants succeed in attracting pollinating insects in various ways. For example, some plants draw the attention of flies with the use of brightly colored petals. Researchers recently found that one plant, *Aristolochia microstoma*, attracts flies by smelling like the dead beetles that some flies lay eggs in. But the plant does more than simply ( **30** ). It temporarily traps them within its flowers; as a fly moves around inside, the pollen on its body spreads onto the plant. The plant also ensures its own pollen gets onto the fly's body so that the insect can pollinate another plant after being released.

The researchers found the plant actually releases the same chemical that gives dead beetles their smell. Because this chemical is rarely found in plants, the researchers believe the plant has evolved specifically to target flies that use dead beetles as egg-laying sites. They also say that ( **31** ). This comes from the fact that the plant's flowers are located among dead leaves and rocks on the ground— exactly where the flies usually search for dead beetles.

(29)
1 Rather
2 In short
3 Nonetheless
4 In exchange

(30)
1 collect dead insects
2 hide its smell from insects
3 trick the flies with its smell
4 provide a safe place for flies

(31)
1 there is further support for this theory
2 the chemical has another purpose
3 the plant is an important food source
4 many insects see the plant as a danger

**3**

*Read each passage and choose the best answer from among the four choices for each question. Then, on your answer sheet, find the number of the question and mark your answer.*

# Fences and Ecosystems

Fences help to divide property and provide security, among other things. They can also affect ecosystems. A study in the journal *BioScience* concluded that fences create both "winners" and "losers" among animal species in the regions in which they are placed. According to the study, generalist species—those that can consume a variety of foods and can survive in multiple habitats—have little problem with physical boundaries. On the other hand, specialist species, which require unique conditions to survive, suffer from being cut off from a particular food source or geographical area. Because specialist species outnumber generalist species, the study found that for every winner, there are multiple losers.

The impact of fences is not limited to ecosystems. In the mid-twentieth century, Botswana in Southern Africa erected fences to address international regulations designed to prevent the spread of a disease affecting cattle. While the fences have helped protect cattle, they have prevented the seasonal movements of animals such as wildebeests and blocked their access to water. The resulting decline in wildebeest populations threatens not only the ecosystem but also the region's wildlife tourism. The government's continued reliance on fences has led to concerns that limiting animal migration will hurt wildlife tourism, which is valuable to Botswana's economy.

The negative ecological effects of fences can be limited by making changes to them to allow certain animals through. Nevertheless, the study's authors believe a more fundamental change is necessary. Eliminating all fences, they say, is not a realistic option; instead, fence planning should be carried out with an eye on the big picture. For example, fences are often constructed to obtain short-term results and then removed, but researchers have found that months—or even years—later, some animals continue to behave as if the fences are still there. Consideration should therefore be given to all aspects of fence design and location to ensure a minimal impact on ecosystems.

*(32)* The study introduced in the first paragraph showed that
1 fences that cross through more than one type of habitat benefit animals more than those built within a single habitat.
2 although fences create many problems, they have less of an effect on the ability of animal populations to survive than previously thought.
3 fences are effective at protecting some species from other harmful species that tend to use up the resources many animals need to survive.
4 although fences are not harmful to some species, they can have serious negative effects on a large number of animals.

*(33)* What is true with regard to the fences that were built in Botswana?
1 The changes that they caused in the migration patterns of animals resulted in the spread of disease among cattle.
2 They could be responsible for indirectly affecting an industry that is important to the country's economy.
3 They are considered necessary in order to increase the safety of tourists who visit the country to see wildlife.
4 The success they have had in reducing disease-spreading species has benefited ecosystems in unexpected ways.

*(34)* What is one reason that careful planning is necessary when constructing fences?
1 Changing the design of a fence after it has been built can actually cause more problems than building a new one.
2 It is possible that fences will continue to have an effect on animals in an area even after the fences have been removed.
3 Putting up multiple fences in a given area without a clear plan beforehand has not stopped animals from entering dangerous areas.
4 The number of animal species that make use of fences to protect themselves from predators has increased.

# The Soccer War

In July 1969, there was a short yet intense war between the Central American countries of El Salvador and Honduras following a series of World Cup qualifying soccer matches they played against each other. Although the conflict is often called the "Soccer War," its causes went far beyond sports.

Honduras is much larger than El Salvador but is far less densely populated. Since the late 1800s, land in El Salvador had been controlled primarily by elite families, which meant there was little space for ordinary farmers. By the 1960s, around 300,000 Salvadorans had entered Honduras illegally to obtain cheap land or jobs. The Honduran government blamed the immigrants for its economic stresses and removed them from their lands, forcing them out of the country. Wealthy Salvadorans feared the negative economic effects of so many immigrants returning home and threatened to overthrow the Salvadoran president if military action was not taken against Honduras. This, combined with border disputes that had existed for many years, brought relations between the countries to a low point.

Tensions were raised further by the media of both countries, which made up or exaggerated stories that fueled their bitterness toward one another. The Salvadoran press accused the Honduran government of cruel and illegal treatment of Salvadoran immigrants, while the Honduran press reported that those same immigrants were committing serious crimes. Such reports were made at the request of the countries' governments: in El Salvador, the goal was to convince the public that military force against its neighbor was necessary, while in Honduras, the government wanted to gain public support for its decision to force Salvadoran immigrants out of the country.

The World Cup qualifying matches were happening at the same time as the migrant situation was intensifying. On the day of the last match, El Salvador accused Honduras of violence against Salvadorans and cut off relations, and within weeks, El Salvador's military attacked Honduras, beginning the war. Historians note that the term Soccer War was misleading. At the time, the United States was part of an alliance with Central American nations, but it chose to stay out of the war. In fact, according to an American diplomat, the inaccurate belief that a sporting event was behind the conflict led the US government to overlook its seriousness. Issues such as land ownership, which were the true origin of the conflict, remained unresolved. This led to continued political and social instability and, ultimately, a civil war in El Salvador in the following decades.

(35) According to the second paragraph, in what way were Salvadoran immigrants to Honduras a cause of the "Soccer War"?
1 El Salvador's president believed the removal of the immigrants from their homes in Honduras was a sign that Honduras was going to attack.
2 The Honduran government began sending poor Hondurans to seek land in El Salvador, causing upset Salvadoran farmers to move to Honduras in response.
3 Rich Salvadorans pressured their government to make war against Honduras after the immigrants were forced out of their homes.
4 The immigrants' constant movement back and forth between the countries created trouble for Honduran border officials.

(36) In the time before the start of the Soccer War, the media in each country
1 attempted to pressure both governments to ensure that the Salvadoran immigrants received better treatment.
2 were prevented by their governments from reporting on illegal acts that were being committed against citizens.
3 put so much emphasis on the soccer rivalry that they failed to report more-important news about illegal acts.
4 were asked by their governments to make up untrue or misleading news stories that made the other country look bad.

(37) What does the author of the passage suggest in the final paragraph?
1 American diplomats still continue to worry that fighting will break out between Honduras and El Salvador again.
2 The terrible effects of the Soccer War made Honduras and El Salvador realize that their actions leading up to the war were wrong.
3 A mistaken belief about the Soccer War meant that its real causes were not recognized, resulting in another conflict.
4 The US government's policies caused many Central American nations to cut off relations, making the conflict in the region worse.

# *Competing against Braille*

Although Braille is the standard writing system for blind people today, this alphabet of raised dots representing letters was not always the only system. Another system, Boston Line Type, was created in the 1830s by Samuel Gridley Howe, a sighted instructor at a US school for blind people. Howe's system utilized the letters in the standard English alphabet used by sighted people, but they were raised so they could be felt by the fingers. Blind students, however, found it more challenging to distinguish one letter from another than they did with Braille. Nevertheless, Howe believed that the fact that reading materials could be shared by both blind and sighted readers outweighed this disadvantage. His system, he argued, would allow blind people to better integrate into society; he thought Braille encouraged isolation because it was unfamiliar to most sighted people.

It gradually became clear that a system using dots was not only easier for most blind people to read but also more practical, as the dots made writing relatively simple. Writing with Boston Line Type required a special printing press, but Braille required only simple, portable tools, and it could also be typed on a typewriter. Still, despite students' overwhelming preference for Braille, Boston Line Type remained in official use in schools for the blind because it allowed sighted instructors to teach without having to learn new sets of symbols. Even when Boston Line Type lost popularity, other systems continued to be introduced, leading to what became known as the "War of the Dots," a situation in which various writing systems competed to become the standard.

One of these, called New York Point, was similar to Braille in that it consisted of raised dots. Its main advantage was that typing it required only one hand. Braille, though, could more efficiently and clearly display capital letters and certain forms of punctuation. There were other candidates as well, and debates about which was superior soon became bitter. Blind people, meanwhile, were severely inconvenienced; books they could read were already in short supply, and the competing systems further limited their options, as learning a new system required great time and effort. At one national convention, a speaker reportedly summed up their frustrations by jokingly suggesting a violent response to the next person who invents a new system of printing for the blind.

The War of the Dots continued into the 1900s, with various groups battling for funding and recognition. In the end, the blind activist Helen Keller was extremely influential in ending the debate. She stated that New York Point's weaknesses in regard to capitalization and punctuation were extremely serious and that reading it was hard on her fingers. Braille won out, and other systems gradually disappeared. Although the War of the Dots interfered with blind people's education for a time, it had a silver lining: the intense battle stimulated the development of various technologies, such as new typewriters, that greatly enhanced blind people's literacy rates and ability to participate in modern society.

*(38)* What did Samuel Gridley Howe believe about Boston Line Type?
   **1** The time it saved blind people in reading made up for the fact that it took much longer to write than Braille.
   **2** The fact that it combined raised dots with other features made it easier for blind people to use it when communicating with one another.
   **3** Although it was difficult for students to learn, the fact that it could be read more quickly than Braille was a major advantage.
   **4** It was worth adopting because of the role it could play in helping blind people to better fit in with people who are able to see.

*(39)* In the second paragraph, what does the author of the passage suggest about Boston Line Type?

**1** Its continued use was not in the best interests of blind people, whose opinions about which system should be used were seemingly not taken into account.

**2** Teachers at schools for the blind convinced students not to use it because they thought systems with fewer dots would be easier for students to read.

**3** Despite it causing the "War of the Dots," its popularity among students was a key factor in the development of other tools for blind people.

**4** It was only successfully used in writing by students in schools for the blind after the introduction of the typewriter.

*(40)* The suggestion by the speaker at the national convention implies that blind people

**1** felt that neither Braille nor the New York Point system could possibly meet the needs of blind readers.

**2** were unhappy that the debates over which system to use were indirectly preventing them from accessing reading materials.

**3** did not like that they were being forced to use a writing system that had not been developed by a blind person.

**4** were starting to think that other types of education had become much more important than learning to read books.

*(41)* What conclusion does the author of the passage make about the War of the Dots?

**1** It was so serious that it is still having a negative influence on the research and development of technology for the blind today.

**2** It would have caused fewer bad feelings if Helen Keller had not decided that she should become involved in it.

**3** It had some positive effects in the long term because the competition led to improvements in the lives of blind people.

**4** It could have been avoided if people in those days had been more accepting of technologies like the typewriter.

**4**

- Write an essay on the given TOPIC.
- Use TWO of the POINTS below to support your answer.
- Structure: introduction, main body, and conclusion
- Suggested length: 120-150 words
- Write your essay in the space provided on Side B of your answer sheet. <u>Any writing outside the space will not be graded.</u>

## TOPIC

*Agree or disagree: The government should do more to promote reusable products*

## POINTS

- Costs
- Effect on businesses
- Garbage
- Safety

# ●一次試験 · Listening Test

| | | There are three parts to this listening test. | | |
|---|---|---|---|---|
| **Part 1** | **Dialogues:** | 1 question each | Multiple-choice |
| **Part 2** | **Passages:** | 2 questions each | Multiple-choice |
| **Part 3** | **Real-Life:** | 1 question each | Multiple-choice |

※ Listen carefully to the instructions.

## Part 1

**No. 1**

1 Get the man to fill in for the receptionist.
2 Ask the man to fire the receptionist.
3 Do the receptionist's job herself.
4 Warn the receptionist about being late.

**No. 2**

1 He has to improve his class performance.
2 He cannot change his work schedule.
3 He will quit his part-time job.
4 He does not go to science class.

**No. 3**

1 He cannot pay his children's college fees.
2 He lives too far from his company.
3 He believes he is being underpaid.
4 He feels unable to leave his current job.

**No. 4**

1 She is frequently given new goals.
2 She is not paid enough for overtime work.
3 Her vacation request was denied.
4 Her report received negative feedback.

**No. 5**

1 She should complete her master's degree next year.
2 She should get some work experience.
3 She can rely on his help for one year.
4 She should save some money first.

**No. 6**

1 Review the website more carefully.
2 Choose the same plan as the man.
3 Request a meeting with personnel.
4 Look for another insurance plan.

**No. 7**

1 He got stuck in heavy traffic.
2 He had trouble with his car.
3 He slept for too long.
4 He got lost on the highway.

**No. 8**

1 Jason's teachers should make more effort.
2 Jason should transfer to a private school.
3 Jason's homework load has increased.
4 Jason should be sent to a tutor.

**No. 9**

1 The man should return to his previous position.
2 She will change her position soon.
3 The man should spend more time at home.
4 She would like to travel for work more.

**No. 10**

1 The station renovations are behind schedule.
2 Her train was more crowded than usual.
3 She had trouble changing trains.
4 The station she always uses was closed.

**No. 11**

1 To keep her mind active.
2 To improve her job skills.
3 To take her mind off work.
4 To get ideas for her fiction writing.

**No. 12**

1 He is an experienced mountain climber.
2 He has not gotten much exercise recently.
3 He wants to take a challenging trail.
4 He dislikes riding in cable cars.

## Part 2

**(A)**

**No. 13**
1 To improve her failing health.
2 To show off her cycling technique.
3 To challenge a gender stereotype.
4 To test a new kind of bicycle.

**No. 14**
1 She helped companies to advertise their products.
2 She made and sold women's clothing.
3 She founded a spring water company.
4 She took jobs that were usually done by men.

**(B)**

**No. 15**
1 The images reminded them of Germany.
2 The images were made by professional artists.
3 The images were believed to bring good luck.
4 The images were painted on strips of fabric.

**No. 16**
1 More people have begun sewing as a hobby.
2 Tourism has increased in some areas.
3 Competition among farms has increased.
4 More barns have been built on farms.

**(C)**

**No. 17**
1 It lasted a little under a century.
2 It led to new discoveries about weather patterns.
3 It had the largest effect on people near volcanoes.
4 It had a global impact on farming.

**No. 18**
1 Europeans in North America started building large cities.
2 Forests expanded across the Americas.
3 The growing global population increased pollution.
4 Disease killed off many trees across Europe.

**(D)**

No. 19
1 The increase in noise caused by growing cities.
2 People's attempts to catch them.
3 The brightness of urban areas.
4 Growing competition with other insects.

No. 20
1 Locate fireflies that are not producing light.
2 Help them to get more funding for research.
3 Use a different type of light around their homes.
4 Make reports on any fireflies they see.

**(E)**

No. 21
1 To study dogs' understanding of words.
2 To study dogs' responses to different voices.
3 To study various ways of training dogs.
4 To study how dogs react to their owners' emotions.

No. 22
1 It was consistent with their owners' reports.
2 It varied depending on the breed of the dog.
3 It was opposite to that of human brains.
4 It increased in response to familiar commands.

**(F)**

No. 23
1 They help people to keep warm in winter.
2 They are useful for storing some vegetables.
3 Their name comes from their shape.
4 They are used to grow vegetables all year round.

No. 24
1 They help to support the local economy.
2 They provide a model for surrounding villages.
3 They help the fishing industry to survive.
4 They were found to contain valuable minerals.

## Part 3

*(G)*

**No. 25**

*Situation:* You have just landed at the airport. You need to get downtown as soon as possible. You are told the following at the information desk.

*Question:* How should you go downtown?

**1** By bus.
**2** By subway.
**3** By taxi.
**4** By light-rail.

*(H)*

**No. 26**

*Situation:* You speak some Italian but want to brush up before your vacation in Italy in three months. You are free on Mondays and Thursdays. A language-school representative tells you the following.

*Question:* Which course should you choose?

**1** Martina's.
**2** Giovanni's.
**3** Teresa's.
**4** Alfredo's.

*(I)*

**No. 27**

*Situation:* You have just arrived at a shopping mall to buy a new business suit. You want to save as much money as you can. You hear the following announcement.

*Question:* Which floor should you go to first?

**1** The first floor.
**2** The second floor.
**3** The third floor.
**4** The fourth floor.

*(J)*

**No. 28**

*Situation:* You and your family are at a theme park. Your children are very interested in animals and nature. You hear the following announcement.

*Question:* Which attraction should you go to?

**1** Lizard Encounter.
**2** Discovery Drive.
**3** Into the Sky.
**4** Dream Fields.

*(K)*

**No. 29**

*Situation:* You want your son to learn a new skill. He already takes swimming lessons after school on Wednesdays. A school administrator makes the following announcement.

*Question:* Who should you speak to?

**1** Mr. Gilbert.
**2** Ms. DeLuca.
**3** Mr. Roth.
**4** Ms. Santos.

# ●二次試験・面接

※本書では出題例として2種類のカードを掲載していますが，本番では1枚のみ渡されます。
※面接委員の質問など，二次試験に関する音声はCDに収録されていません。

## 受験者用問題　カード　A

You have **one minute** to prepare.

This is a story about a president of a small company.
You have **two minutes** to narrate the story.

Your story should begin with the following sentence:
**One day, a company president was walking around the office.**

**No.1**      Please look at the fourth picture.  If you were the company president, what would you be thinking?

Now, Mr. / Ms. _____, please turn over the card and put it down.

**No. 2**      Do you think that salary is the most important factor when choosing a career?

**No. 3**      Are people's opinions too easily influenced by the media?

**No. 4**      Should the government do more to protect workers' rights?

You have **one minute** to prepare.

This is a story about a girl who wanted to learn to skateboard.
You have **two minutes** to narrate the story.

Your story should begin with the following sentence:
**One day, a girl was walking home from school.**

**No.1** Please look at the fourth picture. If you were the girl, what would you be thinking?

Now, Mr. / Ms. ＿＿＿, please turn over the card and put it down.

**No. 2** Is it important for parents to participate in their children's school life?

**No. 3** Is playing sports a good way for young people to develop a strong character?

**No. 4** Do you think international events such as the Olympics can improve relations between nations?

# 準1級

## 2022年度 第2回

| | |
|---|---|
| **一次試験** | 2022.10.9実施 |
| **二次試験** | A日程 2022.11.6実施<br>B日程 2022.11.13実施<br>C日程 2022.11.23実施 |

**一次試験・筆記（90分）**
pp.126〜141

**一次試験・リスニング（約31分）**
pp.142〜147
CD赤-27〜52

**二次試験・面接（約8分）**
pp.148〜151

※解答一覧は別冊p.135
※解答と解説は別冊pp.136〜178

※別冊の巻末についている解答用マークシートを使いましょう。

## 合格基準スコア

- **一次試験**‥‥1792
  （満点2250／リーディング750，リスニング750，ライティング750）
- **二次試験**‥‥512（満点750／スピーキング750）

**1**  To complete each item, choose the best word or phrase from among the four choices.  Then, on your answer sheet, find the number of the question and mark your answer.

*(1)*  **A:** Mom, can you make hamburgers for dinner tonight?
**B:** Yes, but I'll have to take the meat out of the freezer and let it (        ) first.
**1** reckon    **2** thaw    **3** stray    **4** shatter

*(2)*  Jocelyn always reminded her son not to tell lies.  She believed it was important to (        ) a strong sense of honesty in him.
**1** remodel    **2** stumble    **3** overlap    **4** instill

*(3)*  Zara was very angry with her boyfriend, but she forgave him after hearing his (        ) apology.  She was sure that he really was sorry.
**1** detectable    **2** earnest    **3** cumulative    **4** underlying

*(4)*  At first, the Smiths enjoyed their backyard swimming pool, but keeping it clean became such a (        ) that they left it covered most of the time.
**1** bureau    **2** nuisance    **3** sequel    **4** metaphor

*(5)*  Throughout the course of history, many great thinkers were at first (        ) for their ideas before eventually being taken seriously.
**1** saturated    **2** flattered    **3** ingested    **4** ridiculed

*(6)*  At first, the little girl felt (        ) in front of the large audience at the speech contest, but after about a minute she began to feel more confident.
**1** mortal    **2** bashful    **3** pious    **4** concise

*(7)* Typewriters are a (　　) of the past.  They remind us how far technology has advanced since they were common in offices and homes.

**1** jumble　　**2** relic　　**3** fraud　　**4** treaty

*(8)* When the man approached the tiger's cage, the huge animal (　　) deeply.  The man stepped back in fear at the terrifying sound.

**1** sparkled　**2** leered　　**3** disproved　**4** growled

*(9)* Police officers must promise to (　　) the law.  This includes, of course, following the law themselves.

**1** gravitate　**2** detach　　**3** uphold　　**4** eradicate

*(10)* All employees have a (　　) medical checkup every year. Companies are required by law to make sure all their workers do it.

**1** gloomy　　**2** compulsory **3** reminiscent **4** muddled

*(11)* Biology students must learn how cell (　　) works, as this process of a single cell splitting into two is commonly found in nature.

**1** division　　**2** appliance　**3** imposition　**4** longitude

*(12)* After the two companies (　　), several senior employees became unnecessary and lost their jobs.

**1** merged　　**2** posed　　**3** conformed　**4** flocked

*(13)* In order to avoid becoming (　　) while exercising, one should always drink enough water.  The longer the workout, the more water is necessary.

**1** dehydrated　**2** eternal　　**3** punctuated　**4** cautious

*(14)* Ken was always well behaved at home, so his mother was shocked when his teacher said he was one of the most (　　) students in his class.

**1** momentary　**2** miniature　**3** disobedient　**4** invincible

*(15)* The police questioned (　　) at the scene of the crime, hoping someone who had been nearby had seen what happened.

**1** bystanders　**2** reformers　**3** mourners　**4** pioneers

*(16)* Several generals attempted to (　　) the country's prime minister. However, they were unsuccessful, and he remains in power.

**1** irrigate　**2** harmonize　**3** outpace　**4** overthrow

*(17)* Caleb finished a draft of his proposal, so he asked his manager to (　　) it. Unfortunately, she thought it still needed a lot of improvement.

**1** scrub　**2** enchant　**3** prune　**4** evaluate

*(18)* American presidents Thomas Jefferson and John Adams exchanged letters with each other for over 50 years. This (　　) is an important part of American history.

**1** matrimony　　　　　　　**2** federation
**3** horizon　　　　　　　　**4** correspondence

*(19)* During the riot, the town was in a state of (　　). People were out in the streets fighting and breaking windows, and many stores were robbed.

**1** disclosure　**2** admittance　**3** attainment　**4** anarchy

*(20)* The flowers of some plants are actually (　　) and can be used to make salads both more delicious and more visually attractive.

**1** stationary　**2** candid　**3** edible　**4** hideous

*(21)* No one was surprised when the famous scientist made many mistakes during his speech. He is (     ) for his poor speaking skills.

**1** treacherous  **2** momentous  **3** flirtatious  **4** notorious

*(22)* All of Brad's hard work and long hours (     ) when his boss gave him a promotion last month.

**1** paid off  **2** wrote back  **3** chopped up  **4** made over

*(23)* Since the CEO's speech was so vague, it took Gina a while to (     ) to the fact that the company was in serious financial trouble.

**1** fill in  **2** duck out  **3** catch on  **4** give up

*(24)* Each member of the team has a job to do for the new project, but the responsibility for coordinating all of their efforts (     ) the manager.

**1** falls on  **2** squares with  **3** drops by  **4** stacks up

*(25)* The employee tried to (     ) his theft from the company by destroying files and other evidence that proved his guilt.

**1** tuck away  **2** latch onto  **3** cover up  **4** doze off

**2**

*Read each passage and choose the best word or phrase from among the four choices for each blank. Then, on your answer sheet, find the number of the question and mark your answer.*

# Nabta Playa's Stone Circle

Many prehistoric societies constructed stone circles. These were created for various reasons, such as tracking the sun's movement. The oldest such circle known to scientists can be found at Nabta Playa in Egypt. At around 7,000 years old, this circle predates England's Stonehenge—probably the world's best-known prehistoric stone circle—by more than 1,000 years. Nabta Playa's climate is extremely dry today, but this was not always the case. ( **26** ), heavy seasonal rainfall during the period when the circle was built led to the formation of temporary lakes, and these attracted cattle-grazing tribes to the area.

Nabta Playa's first settlers arrived around 10,000 years ago. Archaeologists have uncovered evidence that these settlers created a system of deep wells that gave them access to water year-round, and that they arranged their homes in straight rows and equipped them with storage spaces. They also practiced a religion that focused on the worship of cattle, which were central to their lives. These discoveries are evidence that the settlers ( **27** ).

Research findings show that some of the circle's stones would have lined up with the sun on the longest day of the year around 7,000 years ago. This suggests the circle was used as a calendar. One astrophysicist, however, believes the circle ( **28** ). He points out that the positions of other stones match those of stars in the constellation Orion at the time the circle was built. Because of this, he proposes that the circle was an astrological map showing the positions of stars in the night sky.

(26)
1 On the other hand
2 In fact
3 Despite this
4 Similarly

(27)
1 questioned religious ideas
2 lost interest in raising cattle
3 experienced serious internal conflicts
4 developed a sophisticated society

(28)
1 also had another purpose
2 was created much earlier
3 was originally built elsewhere
4 caused people to avoid the area

# The Good Roads Movement

Beginning in the late nineteenth century, the Good Roads Movement transformed America's landscape, helping to create the nation's system of roads and highways. This movement ( **29** ). While most people today assume that the road system was first developed in response to the needs of automobile drivers, this is a myth. Actually, the demand started mainly with cyclists. The invention of the modern bicycle led to a cycling craze in the 1890s, and millions of Americans wanted better, safer roads to cycle on.

Cyclists began pressuring local governments to improve the quality of roads, which were often poorly maintained and dangerous. At first, the movement was resisted by farmers, who did not want their tax dollars to be spent supporting the leisure activities of cyclists from cities. Gradually, however, farmers ( **30** ). One reason for this was an influential pamphlet called *The Gospel of Good Roads: A Letter to the American Farmer*. It convinced many farmers by emphasizing the benefits of roads, such as making it easier for them to transport their crops to markets.

As automobiles became common, the movement quickly gained momentum. ( **31** ), the invention of the Ford Model T in the early 1900s led to many new drivers, who were also eager for better roads. Millions of these affordable cars were sold, and the increase in drivers put pressure on governments to build more roads and improve the quality of existing ones.

(29)
1 was started by car manufacturers
2 had a surprising origin
3 created disagreement among drivers
4 angered many cyclists

(30)
1 increased their protests
2 started using different roads
3 began to change their minds
4 turned against cyclists

(31)
1 By contrast
2 In particular
3 Nonetheless
4 Therefore

# *Recognizing Faces*

Humans are generally very good at recognizing faces and quickly interpreting their expressions. This is achieved by having specific areas of the brain that specialize in processing facial features. The development of this ability makes sense in terms of evolution, since early humans would have needed to judge, for example, whether those around them were angry and therefore potentially dangerous. One unintended consequence, however, is that people often think they see faces on objects in their environment. People perceive these so-called false faces on a variety of objects, from clouds and tree trunks to pieces of food and electric sockets.

Researchers in Australia recently performed a study to learn more about how the brain processes false faces. Previous studies have revealed that for real faces, people's judgment of what emotion a face is expressing is affected by the faces they have just seen. Seeing a series of happy faces, for example, tends to make people assess the face they next see as expressing happiness. In the Australian study, the researchers showed participants a series of false faces that expressed a particular emotion. They found that, as with real faces, the participants' judgments of the emotions expressed by the false faces were affected by the ones they had just been shown. Based on this finding, the researchers concluded that the brain processes false faces in a way similar to how it processes real ones.

The researchers also noted that any object with features that even loosely resemble the layout of a human face—two eyes and a nose above a mouth—can trigger the brain to assess those features for emotional expression. In other words, the brain's criteria for recognizing a face are general rather than specific. The researchers say this is one reason the brain can assess facial expressions so quickly.

*(32)* In the first paragraph, why does the author of the passage mention objects such as clouds?

**1** To support the idea that people's surroundings can affect how well they are able to judge the emotions of others.

**2** To describe how people who cannot identify faces also have trouble identifying certain other objects.

**3** To help explain that our reactions to everyday objects in our environment are controlled by different areas of the brain.

**4** To provide examples of everyday things on which people imagine they can see faces.

*(33)* Previous studies have shown that

**1** people's judgments about what emotions real faces are expressing are influenced by other real faces they have seen immediately before.

**2** people attach emotional meaning to false faces more quickly than they do to real faces.

**3** people tend to judge the emotions expressed by false faces as happier and more positive than those expressed by real faces.

**4** people take longer to distinguish false faces when the faces are not expressing any emotions.

*(34)* What do the researchers in Australia say about the brain's ability to assess the emotions expressed by faces?

**1** The ability will likely disappear over time as it no longer provides an advantage to humans in terms of survival.

**2** The fact that the brain uses loose criteria to identify faces allows people to quickly judge the emotions faces express.

**3** The brain is only able to accurately identify the emotions faces express if those faces have very specific features.

**4** The evolution of this ability occurred even though it created disadvantages as well as benefits for humans in the past.

# Durians and Giant Fruit Bats

The football-sized durian fruit is well known for its unpleasant smell and creamy, sweet flesh. Known as the "king of fruits," durians are believed to have originated in Borneo, but they are now cultivated more widely, with over half of all durians consumed worldwide being grown in Thailand. Durians have long been popular throughout Southeast Asia, but their popularity is now spreading to other parts of the world. There are hundreds of kinds of durians, but the Musang King variety, which is grown almost exclusively in Malaysia, is one of the most highly valued. Durians contain high levels of vitamins, so they are often promoted for their health benefits, which has led to rising exports. In fact, experts predict there will be a 50 percent increase in shipments from Malaysia to China alone during the next decade. In order to take advantage of this situation, many Malaysian farmers have stopped producing crops such as palm oil in favor of producing durians.

Durian trees are not easy to grow, however. They require regular watering and feeding with fertilizer, and they are highly sensitive to temperature. Furthermore, they do not naturally grow in groves, but rather thrive when grown among other trees and shrubs, so growing them in an orchard as a single crop presents a challenge. Ensuring sufficient pollination of the flowers for the trees to produce a good harvest of fruit is a further difficulty for farmers. One characteristic of durian trees is that their flowers only release pollen at night, so insects such as honeybees that feed during the day do not pollinate them. Animals that are active at night take over the role of pollination, but only about 25 percent of a durian tree's flowers ever get pollinated naturally. Because of this, many farmers resort to the labor-intensive practice of pollinating by hand.

Studies have shown that giant fruit bats are the main natural pollinators of durian flowers. However, these bats are chased away or killed by many farmers, who simply see them as pests because they cause damage and reduce profits by feeding on the fruit. The bats are also threatened as a result of being hunted and sold as food, since there is a belief in some Southeast Asian cultures that eating the bats' meat helps to cure breathing problems. Without educating people about the benefits of giant fruit bats, the bats' numbers may decline further, which could have serious consequences for durian farming.

**(35)** According to the first paragraph, what is true about durian production?

**1** Durians are now mainly grown in Malaysia because there is no longer enough land available to cultivate them in other Southeast Asian countries.

**2** Although durians have been selling well in places where they were traditionally grown, they have yet to gain popularity in other countries.

**3** Premium varieties of durians have been criticized by consumers because they have no more nutritional value than cheaper varieties.

**4** Because of the increasing demand for durians, Malaysian farmers are switching from growing other crops to growing durians.

**(36)** One factor that durian farmers need to consider is that

**1** although durian trees can be grown in almost any warm climate, they do best in areas where there are few other plants growing.

**2** the tendency of durian trees to push out other plants is causing a sharp decline in the number of native plants.

**3** durian trees should be grown in a location where they can be easily found by honeybees and other daytime pollinators.

**4** if durian trees are left alone to be pollinated naturally, the trees are unlikely to produce a large amount of fruit.

**(37)** What is one thing the author of the passage says regarding giant fruit bats?

**1** Durian production might suffer if awareness is not raised about the important role giant fruit bats play in durian flower pollination.

**2** Many people in Southeast Asia have become ill as a result of eating bat meat that was sold illegally at some markets.

**3** Some durian farmers deliberately attract giant fruit bats to their orchards so that they can catch them and sell their meat.

**4** There has been a significant drop in natural pollinators of durian flowers because many giant fruit bats have died from breathing problems.

# The Long Range Desert Group

During World War II, the British fought against Germany and Italy in the deserts of North Africa. Desert warfare was characterized by small battles between troops that were widely spread out, and there was a need to move quickly and at night to avoid both detection and the dangerous daytime heat. The area's vast size and sandy terrain made transporting supplies difficult, and the lack of water severely limited operations.

However, for one British army officer, Major Ralph Bagnold, these harsh conditions presented a strategic opportunity. Having spent years exploring the North African desert before the war, Bagnold knew the terrain well, and he was convinced that a small, highly mobile motorized unit that could observe and track enemy forces would be invaluable. At first, British commanders rejected his proposal to form such a unit, believing airplanes were better suited for such long-range intelligence gathering. Bagnold insisted, however, that gathering information on the ground would be advantageous, and his persistence led to the formation of the Long Range Desert Group (LRDG), with Bagnold as commander, in June 1940.

The LRDG was an unconventional unit from the outset. Usual distinctions between ranks did not apply; officers and regular soldiers were on first-name terms, and they were all expected to perform the same tasks. Rather than seeking men who would fight bravely on the battlefield, Bagnold wanted individuals with great stamina, resourcefulness, and mental toughness—men who could, for example, remain motivated and alert for extended periods despite limited access to drinking water. With specialized trucks adapted to desert conditions, the LRDG's patrols were equipped to operate independently for around three weeks and over a range of more than 1,600 kilometers. All necessary items, such as fuel, ammunition, and food, were carried by the unit, so careful supply planning was extremely important.

The LRDG's work mainly involved traveling deep behind enemy lines to observe their movements. The unit had access to a range of weaponry, and while the men were primarily trained to gather intelligence, they also planted mines and launched attacks against enemy airfields and fuel depots. When the Special Air Service (SAS)— a British army unit formed in 1941 to conduct raids behind enemy lines— suffered heavy casualties after parachuting into enemy territory on its first mission, the LRDG was tasked with bringing back the survivors. The rescue mission was a success, and because of its men's extensive knowledge of the desert, the LRDG was given the responsibility of bringing the SAS to and from all future targets by land, providing both transportation and navigation. This almost certainly helped the SAS accomplish its raids with greater success and fewer casualties.

The LRDG's greatest achievement came in 1943, when the unit found a route that enabled British forces to get around heavily defended enemy lines without being detected, allowing them to attack at weaker points in the defenses. This was a crucial turning point in the campaign in North Africa and contributed greatly to the British victory there. The LRDG went on to make significant contributions to the war effort in Europe until 1945.

(38) Major Ralph Bagnold was able to convince British army commanders that
**1** their soldiers were having limited success on missions in the desert because they were not being supplied with the right resources.
**2** the airplanes being used to fly over enemy territory and make observations in the desert were in need of major improvements.
**3** he could lead a unit of men on missions in the desert despite the fact that he had little experience in such an environment.
**4** using a ground-based unit to gather information about enemy activities in the desert would be an effective strategy.

*(39)* What is true regarding the Long Range Desert Group (LRDG)?

**1** The characteristics of the men chosen for it and the way it operated were different from those of traditional military units.

**2** Because of its limited budget, it had to manage with fewer resources and older weapons than other units.

**3** There were a large number of men in its patrols, so the officers had to have special training in management techniques.

**4** The success of its missions was heavily dependent on the group having supplies sent to it behind enemy lines on a regular basis.

*(40)* Which of the following best describes the relationship between the LRDG and the Special Air Service (SAS)?

**1** The two units were combined so that land and air raids could be performed at the same time.

**2** The similar nature of their operations led to competition between the two units and their unwillingness to assist each other.

**3** The LRDG used its knowledge of the desert to help the SAS improve both the effectiveness and safety of its missions.

**4** The involvement of the SAS in LRDG missions made it more difficult for the LRDG to stay behind enemy lines for long periods of time.

*(41)* According to the author of the passage, what happened in 1943?

**1** A mistake made by the LRDG allowed enemy forces to strengthen their hold on territory that the British hoped to gain.

**2** The transfer of the LRDG to Europe meant the SAS had no choice but to attack enemy forces in a heavily defended area without LRDG support.

**3** The activities of the LRDG made it possible for the British army to gain a significant advantage that led to it defeating enemy forces in the area.

**4** British commanders decided the LRDG would be better put to use defending British-held territory than observing enemy activities.

**4**

- Write an essay on the given TOPIC.
- Use TWO of the POINTS below to support your answer.
- Structure: introduction, main body, and conclusion
- Suggested length: 120-150 words
- Write your essay in the space provided on Side B of your answer sheet. <u>Any writing outside the space will not be graded.</u>

## TOPIC

*Should people trust information on the Internet?*

## POINTS

- *Learning*
- *News*
- *Online shopping*
- *Social media*

| | | | |
|---|---|---|---|
| **There are three parts to this listening test.** | | | |
| **Part 1** | **Dialogues:** | 1 question each | Multiple-choice |
| **Part 2** | **Passages:** | 2 questions each | Multiple-choice |
| **Part 3** | **Real-Life:** | 1 question each | Multiple-choice |

※ Listen carefully to the instructions.

## Part 1

**No. 1**

1 Get a blood test today.
2 Try to eat less for breakfast.
3 Go to lunch with Noah.
4 Have a medical checkup next week.

**No. 2**

1 She needs to take more time off.
2 She should be less concerned about money.
3 She is not ready for so much responsibility.
4 She deserves more pay.

**No. 3**

1 He needs to undergo further tests.
2 He will not be able to play in the game.
3 He needs to find a different form of exercise.
4 He has to stay at the hospital.

**No. 4**

1 Contact the new employee.
2 Speak to the manager.
3 Work the shift herself.
4 Change shifts with him.

**No. 5**

1 Contact the hotel about Internet access.
2 Confirm the meeting schedule.
3 Finish preparing the presentation.
4 Buy a ticket for the flight.

**No. 6**

1 Take a taxi home.
2 Order more wine.
3 Catch the last train home.
4 Walk to the closest bus stop.

**No. 7**

1 Pick up the children from school.
2 Cook dinner for his family.
3 Buy the ingredients for tonight's dinner.
4 Order food from a new restaurant.

**No. 8**

1 He has to pay an unexpected fee.
2 He canceled his insurance policy.
3 He is late for a meeting.
4 The company cannot find his policy number.

**No. 9**

1 The man should not change his major.
2 A career in communications might suit the man better.
3 Graphic design is a good choice for the man.
4 The man is not doing well in class.

**No. 10**

1 Find another online chat tool.
2 Prepare a request for a software upgrade.
3 Get more people to join online meetings.
4 Ask to increase the company's budget.

**No. 11**

1 Go to the plant.
2 Study Spanish.
3 Meet with Barbara.
4 Look for an interpreter.

**No. 12**

1 Radio for an ambulance.
2 Move the woman's car for her.
3 Give the woman a parking ticket.
4 Wait in his police car.

## Part 2

*(A)*

No. 13
1  It could not fly high enough.
2  It was too small and light.
3  It could only fly short distances.
4  It used a rare kind of fuel.

No. 14
1  It was tougher than other planes.
2  It had a new kind of weapon.
3  It could land very quickly.
4  It could drop bombs accurately.

*(B)*

No. 15
1  Water supplies decreased.
2  The air became less polluted.
3  Many people had to leave the island.
4  The number of trees increased.

No. 16
1  How to classify the new ecosystem.
2  What to use the water supply for.
3  Whether native plants should be protected.
4  Where agriculture should be allowed.

*(C)*

No. 17
1  She carried her camera everywhere.
2  She made friends with emergency workers.
3  She lent her camera to the children she took care of.
4  She went to many places as a tourist.

No. 18
1  She became famous early in her career.
2  She mainly took photos at auctions.
3  She held very large exhibitions.
4  She did not show people her photos.

*(D)*

**No. 19**

**1** It does not require the use of fresh water.
**2** It can only be done in certain climates.
**3** It produces a large amount of gas.
**4** It uses less meat than it did in the past.

**No. 20**

**1** The machines it uses are very expensive.
**2** It is damaging to wide areas of land.
**3** It releases chemicals into nearby farmland.
**4** It is frequently dangerous for workers.

*(E)*

**No. 21**

**1** Young people's changing interests.
**2** Young people's increasing need for exercise.
**3** Young people's economic situation.
**4** Young people's passion for nature.

**No. 22**

**1** They are unlikely to survive long.
**2** They do not do well outside of cities.
**3** They rarely employ local people.
**4** They take up too much space.

*(F)*

**No. 23**

**1** Alligators have efficient jaws.
**2** Alligators are related to dinosaurs.
**3** Alligators have muscles in unusual places.
**4** Alligators evolved at the same time as *T. rex.*

**No. 24**

**1** To help with food digestion.
**2** To sense other animals.
**3** To create new blood vessels.
**4** To control their body temperature.

## Part 3

*(G)*
**No. 25**

*Situation:* You are on a plane that has just landed, and you need to catch your connecting flight. A flight attendant is making an announcement.

*Question:* What should you do first after getting off the plane?

**1** Collect your luggage.
**2** Take a bus to another terminal.
**3** Find a gate agent.
**4** Get a new boarding pass printed.

*(H)*
**No. 26**

*Situation:* You want to buy some stick-type incense to burn to help you relax. A store clerk tells you the following.

*Question:* Which incense brand should you buy?

**1** Bouquet Himalaya.
**2** Magnolia's Sanctuary.
**3** Akebono.
**4** Shirley's Gift.

**(I)**

**No. 27**

*Situation:* It is Monday, and you receive a voice mail from a representative at your new Internet provider. You have to work this Thursday from noon to 8 p.m.

*Question:* What should you do?

**1** Reschedule for this weekend.
**2** Reschedule for a weekday next week.
**3** Reschedule for this Thursday morning.
**4** Reschedule for this Friday after 6 p.m.

**(J)**

**No. 28**

*Situation:* You are applying to a college to study psychology. An admissions officer is talking to you about your application.

*Question:* What should you do?

**1** Pay your application fee.
**2** Go to a campus event next week.
**3** Get a letter of recommendation.
**4** Submit your high school records.

**(K)**

**No. 29**

*Situation:* You are on a trip abroad and want to take a free local tour. You get carsick easily. You are told the following at your hotel's information desk.

*Question:* Which tour is the best for you?

**1** The one from 1 p.m.
**2** The one from 2:30 p.m.
**3** The one from 3 p.m.
**4** The one from 5 p.m.

※本書では出題例として2種類のカードを掲載していますが，本番では1枚のみ渡されます。
※面接委員の質問など，二次試験に関する音声はCDに収録されていません。

## 受験者用問題　カード　A

You have **one minute** to prepare.

This is a story about a couple that wanted to save money.
You have **two minutes** to narrate the story.

Your story should begin with the following sentence:
**One day, a woman was talking with her husband.**

**No. 1**    Please look at the fourth picture. If you were the woman, what would you be thinking?

Now, Mr. / Ms. _____, please turn over the card and put it down.

**No. 2**    Do you think it is better to buy a home than to rent a place to live?

**No. 3**    Should Japan increase the amount of green space in its cities?

**No. 4**    Do people these days maintain a good balance between their private lives and their careers?

You have **one minute** to prepare.

This is a story about a couple who lived near the ocean.
You have **two minutes** to narrate the story.

Your story should begin with the following sentence:
**One day, a couple was taking a walk by the beach.**

**No. 1** Please look at the fourth picture. If you were the husband, what would you be thinking?

Now, Mr. / Ms. _____, please turn over the card and put it down.

**No. 2** Do you think Japanese people should express their political opinions more?

**No. 3** Do you think companies should do more to help society?

**No. 4** Is it possible for the actions of individuals to help reduce global warming?

# 準1級

## 2022年度 第❶回

| | |
|---|---|
| **一次試験** | 2022.6.5実施 |
| **二次試験** | A日程 2022.7.3実施<br>B日程 2022.7.10実施<br>C日程 2022.7.17実施 |

**一次試験・筆記(90分)**
pp.154〜169

**一次試験・リスニング(約30分)**
pp.170〜175
CD緑-1〜26

**二次試験・面接(約8分)**
pp.176〜179

※解答一覧は別冊p.179
※解答と解説は別冊pp.180〜222

※別冊の巻末についている解答用マークシートを使いましょう。

## 合格基準スコア

● **一次試験**……1792
（満点2250／リーディング750, リスニング750, ライティング750）
● **二次試験**……512（満点750／スピーキング750）

**1** To complete each item, choose the best word or phrase from among the four choices. Then, on your answer sheet, find the number of the question and mark your answer.

*(1)* After considering the case, the judge decided to show ( ) and only gave the man a warning. She said that he was clearly very sorry for his crime.

**1** disgrace **2** closure **3** mercy **4** seclusion

*(2)* Lisa looks exactly like her twin sister, but she has a completely different ( ). She is very calm and rarely gets angry, unlike her sister.

**1** temperament **2** accumulation
**3** veneer **4** glossary

*(3)* *A:* Annabel, don't just ( ) your shoulders when I ask you if you've finished your homework. Give me a clear answer.
*B:* Sorry, Mom. I'm almost done with it.

**1** echo **2** bow **3** dump **4** shrug

*(4)* When there is a big business convention in town, it is almost impossible to find a hotel with a ( ). Most hotels quickly get fully booked.

**1** sprain **2** segment **3** transition **4** vacancy

*(5)* The detective ( ) the gang member for hours, but he would not say who had helped him commit the crime. Eventually, the detective stopped trying to get information from him.

**1** discharged **2** converted **3** interrogated **4** affiliated

*(6)* To treat an injured ankle, doctors recommend ( ). This can be done by wrapping a bandage tightly around the injury.

**1** depression **2** progression **3** compression **4** suspicion

*(7)*  **A:** It suddenly started raining heavily on my way home, and I got completely wet.
**B:** You should have (          ) my advice and taken an umbrella with you.
**1** molded　　**2** heeded　　**3** twisted　　**4** yielded

*(8)* As a way of attracting more (          ) customers, the perfume company began advertising its products in magazines read mainly by wealthy people.
**1** theatrical　　**2** brutal　　**3** frantic　　**4** affluent

*(9)* The teacher said that, apart from a few (          ) errors, the student's essay was perfect. He gave it the highest score possible.
**1** trivial　　**2** conclusive　　**3** palatial　　**4** offensive

*(10)* The injured soccer player watched (          ) as his replacement played in the final game. He had really wanted to continue playing.
**1** substantially　　　　**2** previously
**3** enviously　　　　　**4** relevantly

*(11)* The new hotel in front of Abraham's apartment building is not tall enough to (          ) his view of the mountains beyond the city. He can still see them clearly.
**1** obstruct　　**2** delegate　　**3** entangle　　**4** boost

*(12)* Having spilled red wine on the white carpet, Martha tried to remove the (          ) with soap and water. However, she could not remove it completely.
**1** stain　　**2** slit　　**3** bump　　**4** blaze

*(13)* The war continued for a year, but neither side could (          ). With victory seemingly impossible, the two countries agreed to stop fighting.
**1** devise　　**2** prevail　　**3** evolve　　**4** reconstruct

*(14)* The leader used the political instability in his country as a (     ) for introducing strict new laws aimed at preventing any opposition to his rule.

**1** trance      **2** downfall      **3** rampage      **4** pretext

*(15)* The suspect continued to (     ) his innocence to the police. He told them repeatedly he had been nowhere near the place where the crime had occurred.

**1** conceal      **2** counter      **3** expire      **4** assert

*(16)* Good writers make every effort to (     ) mistakes from their work, but occasionally they miss some errors and have to make corrections later.

**1** eliminate      **2** expend      **3** stabilize      **4** oppress

*(17)* After the kidnappers returned the child to its parents in exchange for a large (     ), they tried to escape with the money. Police soon caught them, however, and returned the money to the couple.

**1** ransom      **2** applause      **3** monopoly      **4** prank

*(18)* Gaspar applied to go to a (     ) university. Unfortunately, his grades were not good enough, so he had to go to a lesser-known one.

**1** prestigious                    **2** spontaneous
**3** cordial                        **4** petty

*(19)* The spies (     ) themselves as army officers in an attempt to enter the military base without being noticed.

**1** chronicled      **2** disguised      **3** rendered      **4** revitalized

*(20)* Timothy is a very (     ) employee. He is reliable and eager to help, and he always shows loyalty to his company and coworkers.

**1** grotesque      **2** defiant      **3** devoted      **4** feeble

*(21)* To help Paul lose weight, his doctor recommended that he (　　　) his diet. Specifically, she suggested that he eat fewer fatty foods and more fiber.

**1** modify   　　**2** pluck   　　**3** exclaim   　　**4** distill

*(22)* *A:* I've been so busy at work, and now I have to (　　) training our newest employee.

*B:* That's too much. You should ask your boss if someone else can do it instead.

**1** turn over   　　　　　　**2** contend with

**3** prop up   　　　　　　**4** count off

*(23)* The young boy tried to blame his dog for the broken vase. However, his mother did not (　　) the lie and sent him to his room.

**1** fall for   　　**2** hang on   　　**3** see out   　　**4** flag down

*(24)* In his speech, the CEO (　　) his plan for the company's development over the next five years. He hoped this would help guide everyone's work as the company grew.

**1** mapped out   **2** leaped in   　**3** racked up   　**4** spaced out

*(25)* Last year, Harold spent all his money buying shares in various companies. He was (　　) the stock market performing well over the next few years.

**1** casting away   　　　　　**2** putting down

**3** stepping up   　　　　　**4** betting on

*Read each passage and choose the best word or phrase from among the four choices for each blank. Then, on your answer sheet, find the number of the question and mark your answer.*

# The Peter Principle

A theory known as the Peter Principle may explain why there are many people in managerial positions who ( **26** ). According to the theory, employees who perform well in lower-level positions will eventually rise to positions they are not prepared for. The reason for this is that employees generally get promoted based on how well they perform in their current positions. Although this kind of promotion policy may seem logical, failing to fully consider employees' strengths and weaknesses results in them eventually reaching positions for which their abilities are unsuited.

One study examined the careers of salespeople who were promoted to managerial positions. As expected, the study found that the best salespeople were the most likely to receive promotions, but it also found that they performed the worst in managerial roles. The study showed that promoting employees based solely on current performance ( **27** ). Not only do companies end up with poor managers but they also lose their best workers in lower-level positions.

The researchers who carried out the study say that one problem is that companies make the mistake of simply assuming that high-performing employees will naturally be good managers. In most companies, new employees receive specialized training in how to do their jobs. ( **28** ), new managers are often given little or no training. This seems to suggest that one way to lessen the effects of the Peter Principle is to provide proper training for new managers.

*(26)*　**1**　earn lower-than-average salaries
　　　**2**　love their jobs
　　　**3**　have worked for several companies
　　　**4**　perform poorly

*(27)*　**1**　has two disadvantages
　　　**2**　cannot be avoided
　　　**3**　is a gamble worth taking
　　　**4**　prevents creative thinking

*(28)*　**1**　Of course
　　　**2**　On the other hand
　　　**3**　What is more
　　　**4**　For a similar reason

# Nearsightedness

Nearsightedness has been increasing around the world at a rapid rate. People with this condition can see objects that are close to them clearly, but objects that are far away appear blurry. Many people blame this trend on the use of digital screens. They claim that using devices such as computers and smartphones leads to eyestrain, and that blue light, which is produced by digital screens, damages light-sensitive cells in the back of the eye. However, there is no clear evidence that digital screens ( **29** ).

In fact, the rise in nearsightedness began before digital screens became widely used. Some research suggests that the real issue is that people ( **30** ). This results in a lack of exposure to natural light. Nearsightedness is caused by the stretching of the lens in the eye, which reduces its ability to focus light. However, the release of dopamine, a chemical produced by the brain, can prevent this from occurring, and exposure to natural light leads to greater dopamine production.

Some experts say that being outdoors for about three hours a day can help prevent nearsightedness. For many people, however, doing this is impossible due to school and work schedules. ( **31** ), it may be more practical for people to change the kind of lighting they use in their homes. There is already lighting available that provides some of the benefits of natural light, and it is hoped that research will provide more alternatives in the future.

(29)
1 have long-term effects on eyesight
2 can help solve the problem
3 can be used on all devices
4 will improve in the future

(30)
1 sit too close to their screens
2 rely too much on vision
3 spend too much time indoors
4 fail to do enough physical exercise

(31)
1 In the same way
2 For example
3 Despite this
4 Instead

*Read each passage and choose the best answer from among the four choices for each question. Then, on your answer sheet, find the number of the question and mark your answer.*

# Honey Fungus

The largest living organism on Earth is not a whale or other large animal. Rather, it belongs to the group of organisms which includes mushrooms and toadstools. It is a type of fungus commonly known as honey fungus, and its rootlike filaments spread underground throughout a huge area of forest in the US state of Oregon. DNA testing has confirmed that all the honey fungus in the area is from the same organism, and, based on its annual rate of growth, scientists estimate it could be over 8,000 years old. They also calculate that it would weigh around 35,000 tons if it were all gathered together.

As impressive as this honey fungus is, it poses a problem for many trees in the forest. The fungus infects the trees and absorbs nutrients from their roots and trunks, often eventually killing them. Unfortunately, affected trees are usually difficult to spot, as the fungus hides under their bark, and its filaments are only visible if the bark is removed. In the late fall, the fruiting bodies of the fungus appear on the outside of the trees, but only for a few weeks before winter. Although the trees attempt to resist the fungus, they usually lose the battle in the end because the fungus damages their roots, preventing water and nutrients from reaching their upper parts.

Full removal of the honey fungus in Oregon has been considered, but it would prove to be too costly and time-consuming. Another solution currently being researched is the planting of tree species that can resist the fungus. Some experts have suggested, however, that a change of perspective may be necessary. Rather than viewing the effects of the honey fungus in a negative light, people should consider it an example of nature taking its course. Dead trees will ultimately be recycled back into the soil, benefiting the area's ecosystem.

*(32)* According to the passage, what is one thing that is true about the honey fungus in Oregon?

**1** It is a combination of different mushroom species that started to grow together over time.

**2** It grew slowly at first, but it has been expanding more rapidly in the last thousand years.

**3** It shares the nutrients it collects with the trees and other types of plant life that it grows on.

**4** It is a single organism that has spread throughout a wide area by growing and feeding on trees.

*(33)* Honey fungus is difficult to find because

**1** the mushrooms it produces change color depending on the type of tree that it grows on.

**2** it is generally not visible, except when it produces fruiting bodies for a short time each year.

**3** not only does it grow underground, but it also has an appearance that is like that of tree roots.

**4** it is only able to survive in areas that have the specific weather conditions it needs to grow.

*(34)* What do some experts think?

**1** People should regard the honey fungus's effects on trees as a natural and beneficial process.

**2** The only practical way to deal with the honey fungus is to invest more time and money in attempts to remove it.

**3** Trees that have been infected by the honey fungus can be used to prevent it from spreading further.

**4** The honey fungus can be harvested to provide people with an excellent source of nutrients.

# Intentional Communities

For hundreds of years, people have formed self-sustaining communities, often referred to as intentional communities, which are characterized by shared ideals, collective ownership, and common use of property. The first known intentional community was established in the sixth century BC by a Greek philosopher. Over the following centuries, a number of such communities were created by religious groups wishing to live outside mainstream society. Some of these, such as Christian monasteries and the collective farms called kibbutzim in Israel, remained successful for generations, while others lasted only a few years.

In the twentieth century, philosophical idealism, as seen in the back-to-the-land movement of the 1960s and 1970s, also motivated people to form intentional communities. By the early 1970s, it has been estimated that there were thousands of such communities in the United States alone, though many of those later disbanded. The Foundation for Intentional Communities now lists fewer than 800 communities in the United States and just under 250 in the rest of the world. Intentional communities that failed generally faced a similar challenge. Some people who came to stay were committed to ideals of shared work, growing their own food, and living collectively, but others were less serious. A cofounder of one community recalled, "We had an impractical but noble vision that was constantly undermined by people who came just to play."

Not all intentional communities are destined to fall apart, however. The ongoing success of Damanhur, a spiritual and artistic collective near Turin, Italy, is attributed to open communication and a practical approach. Damanhur organizes its members into family-like groups of 15 to 20 people. The community has found that creating intimacy becomes difficult if a "family" has more than 25 people. In contrast, when there are too few people in the "family," there is not enough collective knowledge to allow for effective decision-making. Damanhur's ideals, which are outlined in its constitution, are upheld by elected leaders, and tensions in the community are handled by holding playful mock battles where people fight with paint-filled toy guns.

It seems that all successful intentional communities share a common trait: the ability to constantly think ahead. As one Damanhur member put it, "You should change things when they work—not when they don't work." This strategy of making changes before problems occur has worked well for Damanhur and other successful communities, which suggests it is an effective way for intentional communities to fulfill the needs of their members in the long term.

*(35)* A common issue faced by intentional communities that failed was that
    **1** a majority of the community was in favor of someone joining, but a small number of individuals opposed it.
    **2** people joined the community with genuine interest, but they lacked the skills or knowledge to contribute effectively.
    **3** some members worked hard to follow the community's ideals, while others took a more casual approach to communal living.
    **4** the community set out to complete an ambitious project, but it could not complete it because of a lack of knowledge and financial resources.

*(36)* What is true of the social structure at Damanhur?
    **1** "Families" are free to create their own rules and do not necessarily have to follow the rules contained in the community's constitution.
    **2** The number of people in a "family" is controlled to create the best conditions for resolving group issues and maintaining good relationships.
    **3** The mock battles that are intended to solve disagreements sometimes become serious and result in some members leaving their "families."
    **4** The community contains "families" of different sizes so that members can choose whether to live in a large or a small group setting.

*(37)* According to the passage, how is Damanhur similar to other successful intentional communities?
    **1** Members of the community are allowed to exchange their responsibilities from time to time to prevent them from becoming exhausted.
    **2** The type of work the community does to earn income changes periodically so that members can learn new skills.
    **3** Members of the community take turns carrying out maintenance on the buildings and equipment that are owned collectively.
    **4** The community continually finds ways to satisfy the needs of its members rather than simply reacting to problems when they arise.

# The British in India

Established in 1600, the British-owned East India Company was one of the world's largest corporations for more than two centuries. By trading overseas with various countries, such as India and China, it was able to import luxury items from these countries into Britain. The British government received a portion of the company's vast profits, so it was more than willing to provide political support. Due to its size, power, and resources, which included a private army of hundreds of thousands of Indian soldiers, the company pressured India into accepting trade contracts that, in general, were only of benefit to the company. After winning a battle against a local ruler in the 1750s, the company seized control of one of the wealthiest provinces in India. As a result, the East India Company was no longer solely acting as a business but also as a political institution, and it began forcing Indian citizens to pay it taxes.

The East India Company gained a reputation among the countries it did business with for being untrustworthy. It also started to lose popularity within the British Parliament because the company's dishonest trading habits damaged foreign relations with China. Then, in the 1850s, angered by the way they were being treated, a group of soldiers in the East India Company's army rebelled. They marched to Delhi to restore the Indian emperor to power, and their actions caused rebellion against the British to spread to other parts of India. The rebellion was eventually brought under control after about two years, but it triggered the end of the East India Company. The British government, which blamed the East India Company for allowing the rebellion to happen, took control of India, and an era of direct British rule began. The British closed down the East India Company, removed the Indian emperor from power, and proceeded to rule India for almost a century.

While some claim that India benefited from British rule, typically using the construction of railways as an example, many historians argue that the country was negatively affected. In an effort to reinforce notions that British culture was superior, Indians were educated to have the same opinions, morals, and social preferences as the British.

The British also implemented a policy known as "divide and rule," which turned Indians from different religious backgrounds against each other.  The British government used this strategy to maintain its control over India, as members of these religions had joined forces during the earlier rebellion.  However, nationalist feelings among Indians increased from the early 1900s, and India eventually gained its independence in the late 1940s.

Although the East India Company stopped operating more than a century ago, it has had a lasting influence.  Some experts say it pioneered the concept of multinational corporations and ultimately led to the economic system of capitalism that is widespread today.  Moreover, the connection between the British government and the East India Company set a precedent for using political power to help achieve business objectives.

*(38)* What was one result of India doing business with the East India Company?

**1** India could afford to increase the size of its military because it was able to make trade deals with other countries.

**2** India had little choice but to agree to business agreements that were unfavorable to it.

**3** The Indian government needed to raise taxes in order to pay for losses from failed trade contracts.

**4** The Indian government's relationship with China became worse, which almost resulted in a break in trade between the two countries.

*(39)* What led to the British government taking control of India?
**1** The British government held the East India Company responsible for an uprising that occurred.
**2** The Indian people voted for British rule after losing confidence in the Indian emperor's ability to rule the country effectively.
**3** The Indian people asked for the help of the British in preventing a war between India and China.
**4** The Indian emperor decided to join forces with the British as a political strategy to maintain control of India.

*(40)* One effect that British rule had on India was that
**1** Indians were able to take part in the process of building a government that reflected their economic and social needs.
**2** schools made an effort to educate their students to have an awareness of both Indian and British cultures.
**3** divisions were created between different groups of Indians to prevent them from challenging British rule.
**4** many of the railroads and other transportation systems built by the Indian government were destroyed.

*(41)* What does the author of the passage say about the East India Company?
**1** The company prevented the British government from achieving its aim of expanding its rule to other countries in Asia.
**2** While the company may have been successful during its time, its business model would not be effective in today's economy.
**3** Although the company no longer exists, it has had a large impact on the present-day global economic landscape.
**4** If the company had never been established, another one would likely have ended up having similar political and economic influence.

**4**

- Write an essay on the given TOPIC.
- Use TWO of the POINTS below to support your answer.
- Structure: introduction, main body, and conclusion
- Suggested length: 120-150 words
- Write your essay in the space provided on Side B of your answer sheet. <u>Any writing outside the space will not be graded.</u>

## TOPIC

*Should people's salaries be based on their job performance?*

## POINTS

● *Age*
● *Company profits*
● *Motivation*
● *Skills*

# ●一次試験・Listening Test

**There are three parts to this listening test.**

| Part 1 | **Dialogues:** | 1 question each | Multiple-choice |
| Part 2 | **Passages:** | 2 questions each | Multiple-choice |
| Part 3 | **Real-Life:** | 1 question each | Multiple-choice |

※ Listen carefully to the instructions.

## Part 1

**No. 1**

1 He no longer drives to work.
2 His car is being repaired.
3 He cannot afford to buy gas.
4 His new bicycle was stolen.

**No. 2**

1 He wants to move out.
2 He likes to have parties.
3 He is not very open.
4 He is very messy.

**No. 3**

1 The other candidates were more qualified.
2 He forgot to call the manager yesterday.
3 The manager did not like him.
4 He missed the interview.

**No. 4**

1 The woman needs to pass it to graduate.
2 It does not match the woman's goals.
3 It is too advanced for the woman.
4 Passing it could help the woman find a job.

**No. 5**

1 The woman should take a break from school.
2 Working as a server is physically demanding.
3 Restaurant workers do not make much money.
4 Students should not get part-time jobs.

**No. 6**

1 Buy a gift from the list.
2 Decline the wedding invitation.
3 Speak to Carla and Antonio.
4 Return the silver dining set.

**No. 7**

1 It has large portions.
2 It is a short drive from home.
3 It is cheaper than other places.
4 It has a good reputation.

**No. 8**

1 Spend time hiking.
2 Go fishing at a lake.
3 Take a ski trip.
4 Go sightseeing.

**No. 9**

1 Some customers complained about it.
2 One of the posts needs to be revised.
3 Kenneth should not edit the latest post.
4 It should be updated more frequently.

**No. 10**

1 Her wallet is missing.
2 Her train pass expired.
3 She missed her train.
4 She wasted her money.

**No. 11**

1 She did not like the pianist's playing.
2 She arrived at the concert late.
3 She could not focus on the concert.
4 She was unable to find her ticket.

**No. 12**

1 Call him back in the evening.
2 Give him new delivery instructions.
3 Change her delivery option online.
4 Tell him what time she will be home.

## Part 2

*(A)*

**No. 13**
  **1** Water levels have decreased in many of them.
  **2** Laws to protect them need to be stricter.
  **3** Countries sharing them usually have the same usage rights.
  **4** They often make it difficult to protect borders.

**No. 14**
  **1** To suggest a solution to a border problem.
  **2** To suggest that poor nations need rivers for electricity.
  **3** To show that dams are often too costly.
  **4** To show how river usage rights can be complicated.

*(B)*

**No. 15**
  **1** It could be used as a poison.
  **2** It was tested on snakes.
  **3** It was difficult to make.
  **4** It was the first medical drug.

**No. 16**
  **1** It took many days to make.
  **2** Only small amounts could be made daily.
  **3** Production was very loosely regulated.
  **4** People there could watch it being made.

*(C)*

**No. 17**
  **1** They hunted only spirit bears with black fur.
  **2** They tried to keep spirit bears a secret.
  **3** They thought spirit bears were dangerous.
  **4** They believed spirit bears protected them.

**No. 18**
  **1** It is easier for them to catch food.
  **2** They are less sensitive to the sun.
  **3** It is harder for hunters to find them.
  **4** Their habitats are all well-protected.

*(D)*

**No. 19**
1 They generate power near where the power is used.
2 They are preferred by small businesses.
3 They do not use solar energy.
4 They are very expensive to maintain.

**No. 20**
1 Governments generally oppose its development.
2 Energy companies usually do not profit from it.
3 It can negatively affect property values.
4 It often pollutes community water sources.

*(E)*

**No. 21**
1 Caring for them costs too much money.
2 They are too difficult to capture.
3 They suffer from serious diseases.
4 They rarely live long after being caught.

**No. 22**
1 Zoos need to learn how to breed them.
2 Governments must make sure laws are followed.
3 They must be moved to new habitats.
4 Protecting them in the wild is not possible.

*(F)*

**No. 23**
1 They are more numerous than is typical.
2 They are similar to those of a distant area.
3 They are the largest in the region.
4 They include images of Europeans.

**No. 24**
1 To indicate certain times of the year.
2 To warn enemies to stay away.
3 To show the way to another settlement.
4 To provide a source of light.

## Part 3

**(G)**
**No. 25**

*Situation:* You want to feed your parrot, Toby, but cannot find his pet food. You check your cell phone and find a voice mail from your wife.

*Question:* Where should you go to find Toby's food?

**1** To the kitchen.
**2** To the living room.
**3** To the front door.
**4** To the garage.

**(H)**
**No. 26**

*Situation:* You want to read a book written by the author Greta Bakken. You want to read her most popular book. A bookstore clerk tells you the following.

*Question:* Which book should you buy?

**1** *The Moon in Budapest.*
**2** *Along That Tree-Lined Road.*
**3** *Mixed Metaphors.*
**4** *Trishaws.*

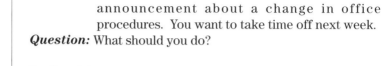

**(I)**
**No. 27**

*Situation:* Your company's president is making an announcement about a change in office procedures. You want to take time off next week.

*Question:* What should you do?

**1** Speak to your manager.
**2** Submit a request on the new website.
**3** E-mail the members of your department.
**4** Contact ABC Resource Systems.

**(J)**
**No. 28**

*Situation:* Your professor is showing your class a course website. You want to get extra credit to improve your grade.

*Question:* What should you do?

**1** Submit an extra research paper through the website.
**2** Complete additional reading assignments.
**3** Create an online resource for the class.
**4** Sign up for a lecture via the news section.

**(K)**
**No. 29**

*Situation:* You are a writer for a newspaper. You arrive home at 8:30 p.m. and hear the following voice mail from your editor. You need two more days to finish your column.

*Question:* What should you do?

**1** Send the file to Bill.
**2** Send the file to Paula.
**3** Call Bill's office phone.
**4** Call Bill on his smartphone.

# ●二次試験・面接

※本書では出題例として2種類のカードを掲載していますが，本番では1枚のみ渡されます。
※面接委員の質問など，二次試験に関する音声はCDに収録されていません。

## 受験者用問題　カード　A

You have **one minute** to prepare.

This is a story about a mayor who wanted to help her town.
You have **two minutes** to narrate the story.

Your story should begin with the following sentence:
**One day, a mayor was having a meeting.**

**No. 1**      Please look at the fourth picture.  If you were the mayor, what would you be thinking?

Now, Mr. / Ms. _____, please turn over the card and put it down.

**No. 2**      Do you think people should spend more time outdoors to learn about nature?

**No. 3**      Should companies provide workers with more vacation days?

**No. 4**      Should the government do more to protect endangered animals?

You have **one minute** to prepare.

This is a story about a woman who wanted to advance her career.
You have **two minutes** to narrate the story.

Your story should begin with the following sentence:
**One day, a woman was talking with her company's CEO in the office.**

**No. 1**      Please look at the fourth picture. If you were the woman, what would you be thinking?

Now, Mr. / Ms. _____, please turn over the card and put it down.

**No. 2**      Are parents too protective of their children these days?

**No. 3**      Does the fast pace of modern life have a negative effect on people?

**No. 4**      Do you think the birth rate in Japan will stop decreasing in the future?

# 準1級

## 2021年度 第3回

一次試験　2022.1.23実施

二次試験　A日程　2022.2.20実施
　　　　　B日程　2022.2.27実施
　　　　　C日程　2022.3.6実施

一次試験・筆記（90分）
　　　　　　pp.182〜197

一次試験・リスニング（約30分）
　　　　　　pp.198〜203
　　　　　　CD緑-27〜52

二次試験・面接（約8分）
　　　　　　pp.204〜207

※解答一覧は別冊p.223
※解答と解説は別冊pp.224〜266

※別冊の巻末についている解答用マークシートを使いましょう。

## 合格基準スコア

● 一次試験⋯1792
　（満点2250／リーディング750, リスニング750, ライティング750）
● 二次試験⋯512（満点750／スピーキング750）

**1** To complete each item, choose the best word or phrase from among the four choices. Then, on your answer sheet, find the number of the question and mark your answer.

*(1)* Roberto was a true (　　　), so he immediately volunteered to join the army when his country was attacked by its neighbor.

**1** villain　　**2** patriot　　**3** spectator　　**4** beggar

*(2)* "Let's take a break now," said the chairperson. "We'll (　　　) the meeting in about 15 minutes to talk about the next item on the agenda."

**1** parody　　**2** resume　　**3** impede　　**4** erect

*(3)* The first time Dan tried skiing, he found it difficult, but on each (　　　) ski trip, he got better. Now he is an expert skier.

**1** sufficient　　**2** arrogant　　**3** subsequent　　**4** prominent

*(4)* The professor is an expert in his field but his (　　　) behavior is a source of embarrassment to his colleagues. "He's always doing or saying strange things," said one.

**1** secular　　**2** eccentric　　**3** vigilant　　**4** apparent

*(5)* Because the vegetable stand was unable to (　　　) that the vegetables it sold were organic, Eddie refused to buy them. It was his strict policy to eat only organic foods.

**1** diverge　　**2** certify　　**3** evade　　**4** glorify

*(6)* As a school guidance counselor, Ms. Pereira specializes in helping students find their (　　　). She believes people should have careers that fit their personality and skills.

**1** boredom　　**2** vocation　　**3** insult　　**4** publicity

*(7)* The marathon runner was so thirsty after the race that she drank a large sports drink in just a few ( ) and then quickly asked for another one.
**1** herds **2** lumps **3** gulps **4** sacks

*(8)* The sleeping baby was ( ) by the loud music coming from her brother's room. She woke up crying, and it took a long time before she fell asleep again.
**1** startled **2** improvised **3** prolonged **4** tolerated

*(9)* *A:* I've been living in this apartment for a year now, and the ( ) is about to end. I have to decide if I should stay or move.
*B:* If your rent will be the same, I recommend renewing your contract and staying.
**1** token **2** lease **3** vicinity **4** dialect

*(10)* The presidential candidate blamed the ( ) economy on the current president. He promised he would improve it if he were elected.
**1** bulky **2** functional **3** ethnic **4** sluggish

*(11)* *A:* Annie, how have you been? Did you enjoy your trip to Italy last year?
*B:* I did, Pablo. Actually, I loved it so much that I've been ( ) moving there. I'd have to wait until my son graduates from high school, though.
**1** contemplating **2** emphasizing
**3** vandalizing **4** illustrating

*(12)* All the senators said they supported the new law, so it was no surprise when they voted for it ( ).
**1** unanimously **2** abnormally **3** mockingly **4** savagely

*(13)* *A:* Did you go to Professor Markham's lecture?
*B:* I did, but it was so boring I could only ( ) it for 15 minutes. After that, I left and went to a café.
**1** execute **2** discern **3** endure **4** relay

*(14)* Houses built in cold regions can be surprisingly (          ) during the winter. Fireplaces, wood furniture, and nice carpets give the homes a warm, comfortable feeling.

**1** rigid          **2** rash          **3** cozy          **4** clumsy

*(15)* Mrs. Wilson was angry when her son broke the window, but she was more disappointed that he tried to (          ) her by telling her that someone else had done it.

**1** pinpoint          **2** suppress          **3** reroute          **4** deceive

*(16)* After Wanda was late for the third time in one month, her manager had a long talk with her about the importance of (          ).

**1** congestion          **2** drainage          **3** optimism          **4** punctuality

*(17)* The young author decided not to follow (          ) storytelling rules and wrote his novel in a unique style.

**1** vulnerable          **2** clueless          **3** conventional          **4** phonetic

*(18)* The items in the box were packaged carefully because they were (          ), but some of them were still damaged when they were being delivered.

**1** coarse          **2** fragile          **3** immovable          **4** glossy

*(19)* The queen (          ) her adviser to the palace, but she became extremely angry when he took a long time to arrive.

**1** summoned          **2** hammered          **3** mingled          **4** trembled

*(20)* The general knew his troops were losing the battle, so he ordered them to (          ). Once they were safely away from the battlefield, he worked on a new plan to defeat the enemy.

**1** entrust          **2** discard          **3** strangle          **4** retreat

*(21)* After Bill began university, he quickly realized that he did not have the (          ) to study advanced math, so he changed his major to geography.

**1** capacity     **2** novelty     **3** bait     **4** chunk

*(22)* The police officer was shocked when his partner suggested they (          ) a suspect in order to force him to admit he had stolen money. Using violence in this way was not allowed.

**1** rough up     **2** give out     **3** break up     **4** take over

*(23)* Julius was lucky to see a rare eagle on his first day of bird-watching. However, 20 years (          ) before he saw another one.

**1** held out     **2** went by     **3** laid off     **4** cut off

*(24)* **A:** Are you going to cancel your weekend beach trip? There's a typhoon coming.
**B:** We haven't (          ) going yet. It depends on which direction the typhoon moves in.

**1** ruled out           **2** stood down
**3** dragged into       **4** scooped up

*(25)* Jun always saved as much money as possible so he would have something to (          ) if he lost his job.

**1** look up to         **2** fall back on
**3** come down with    **4** do away with

*Read each passage and choose the best word or phrase from among the four choices for each blank. Then, on your answer sheet, find the number of the question and mark your answer.*

# Donor Premiums

In recent years, it has become common for charities to give donor premiums—small gifts such as coffee mugs—to people who donate money to them. Many charities offer them, and it is widely believed that people give more when they receive donor premiums. However, researchers say that donor premiums tend to ( **26** ). Most people initially give money because they want to make the world a better place or help those who are less fortunate. When they receive gifts, though, people can start to become motivated by selfishness and desire. In fact, they may become less likely to donate in the future.

There may, however, be ways to avoid this problem. Research has shown that telling people they will receive gifts after making donations is not the best way to ensure they will contribute in the future. In one study, donors responded better to receiving gifts when they did not expect them. ( **27** ), future donations from such people increased by up to 75 percent. On the other hand, donors who knew that they would receive a gift after their donation did not value the gift highly, regardless of what it was.

Donor premiums may also have indirect benefits. Experts say gifts can ( **28** ). Items such as fancy shopping bags with charity logos, for example, signal that a donor is part of an exclusive group. Such gifts not only keep donors satisfied but also increase the general public's awareness of charities.

*(26)* **1** use up charities' resources
**2** change donors' attitudes
**3** encourage people to donate more
**4** improve the public's image of charities

*(27)* **1** Instead
**2** Nevertheless
**3** In contrast
**4** Furthermore

*(28)* **1** help promote charities
**2** easily be copied
**3** have undesirable effects
**4** cause confusion among donors

# Government Policy and Road Safety

Traffic-related deaths have declined in the United States due to the introduction of safety measures such as seat belts. Many critics of government policy claim, however, that fatalities could be further reduced with stricter government regulation. In fact, some say current government policies regarding speed limits may ( **29** ). This is because speed limits are often set using the "operating speed method." With this method, speed limits are decided based on the speeds at which vehicles that use the road actually travel, and little attention is paid to road features that could increase danger. Unfortunately, this means limits are sometimes set at unsafe levels.

Critics also point out that the United States is behind other nations when it comes to vehicle-safety regulations. In the United States, safety regulations are ( **30** ). Although some vehicles have become larger and their shape has changed, laws have not changed to reflect the increased danger they pose to pedestrians. Critics say that regulating only the safety of vehicle occupants is irresponsible, and that pedestrian deaths have increased even though there are simple measures that could be taken to help prevent them.

One measure for improving road safety is the use of cameras at traffic signals to detect drivers who fail to stop for red lights. Many such cameras were installed in the 1990s and have been shown to save lives. ( **31** ), the number of such cameras has declined in recent years. One reason for this is that there is often public opposition to them due to privacy concerns.

(29)
1 further support this trend
2 reduce seat-belt use
3 encourage dangerous driving
4 provide an alternative solution

(30)
1 designed to protect those inside vehicles
2 opposed by many drivers
3 actually being decreased
4 stricter for large vehicles

(31)
1 For instance
2 Likewise
3 Despite this
4 Consequently

# Caligula

The Roman emperor Caligula, also known as the "mad emperor," became so infamous that it is difficult to separate fact from legend regarding his life. During his reign, Caligula suffered what has been described as a "brain fever." It has often been said that this illness caused him to go insane, a claim that is supported by his seemingly irrational behavior following his illness. Today, however, some historians argue that his actions may have been a deliberate part of a clever, and horribly violent, political strategy.

After his illness, Caligula began torturing and putting to death huge numbers of citizens for even minor offenses. He also claimed to be a living god. These actions may suggest mental instability, but another explanation is that they were intended to secure his position. While Caligula was ill, plans were made to replace him, since he had not been expected to survive, and he likely felt betrayed and threatened as a result. Similarly, while claiming to be a god certainly sounds like a symptom of insanity, many Roman emperors were considered to become gods upon dying, and Caligula may have made the claim to discourage his enemies from assassinating him.

The story of how Caligula supposedly tried to appoint his horse Incitatus to a powerful government position is also sometimes given as evidence of his mental illness. However, Caligula is said to have frequently humiliated members of the Roman Senate, making them do things such as wearing uncomfortable clothing and running in front of his chariot. Elevating his horse to a position higher than theirs would have been another way to make the Senate members feel worthless. Eventually, though, Caligula's behavior went too far, and he was murdered. Efforts were made to erase him from history, leaving few reliable sources for modern historians to study. As a result, it may never be known whether he truly was the mad emperor.

*(32)* Some modern historians argue that
  **1**  Caligula's seemingly crazy actions may actually have been part of a carefully thought-out plan.
  **2**  the "brain fever" that Caligula suffered was more serious than it was originally believed to be.
  **3**  Caligula should not be judged based on the period when he was suffering from a mental illness.
  **4**  many of the violent acts that Caligula is reported to have carried out were performed by other Roman emperors.

*(33)* What may have been one result of Caligula's illness?
  **1**  The fact that he almost died caused him to stop being interested in anything except gods and religion.
  **2**  He felt that he could no longer trust anyone, leading him to change the way he governed.
  **3**  Roman citizens thought he was still likely to die, so he attempted to show them that the gods would protect him.
  **4**  He began to doubt old beliefs about Roman emperors, which led to serious conflicts with other members of the government.

*(34)* According to the passage, how did Caligula feel about the members of the Roman Senate?
  **1**  He felt the people should respect them more, since they would do anything to protect him from his enemies.
  **2**  He wanted to show his power over them, so he often found ways to make them feel they had no value.
  **3**  He disliked them because he felt that they were physically weak and had poor fashion sense.
  **4**  He was grateful for their support, so he held events such as chariot races in order to honor them.

# The Friends of Eddie Coyle

In 1970, American writer George V. Higgins published his first novel, *The Friends of Eddie Coyle*. This crime novel was inspired by the time Higgins spent working as a lawyer, during which he examined hours of police surveillance tapes and transcripts in connection with the cases he was involved in. What he heard and read was the everyday speech of ordinary criminals, which sounded nothing like the scripted lines of TV crime dramas at the time. Higgins learned how real criminals spoke, and their unique, often messy patterns of language provided the basis for *The Friends of Eddie Coyle*. The novel's gritty realism was far removed from the polished crime stories that dominated the bestseller lists at the time. Higgins neither glamorized the lives of his criminal characters nor portrayed the police or federal agents in a heroic light.

One aspect that distinguishes *The Friends of Eddie Coyle* from other crime novels is that it is written almost entirely in dialogue. Given the crime genre's reliance on carefully plotted stories that build suspense, this was a highly original approach. Important events are not described directly, instead being introduced through conversations between characters in the novel. Thus, readers are given the sense that they are secretly listening in on Eddie Coyle and his criminal associates. Even action scenes are depicted in dialogue, and where narration is necessary, Higgins writes sparingly, providing only as much information as is required for readers to follow the plot. The focus is primarily on the characters, the world they inhabit, and the codes of conduct they follow.

Although Higgins's first novel was an immediate hit, not all readers liked the author's writing style, which he also used in his following books. Many complained that his later novels lacked clear plots and contained too little action. Yet Higgins remained committed to his belief that the most engaging way to tell a story is through the conversations of its characters, as this compels the reader to pay close attention to what is being said. Despite writing many novels, Higgins was never able to replicate the success of his debut work. Toward the end of his life, he became disappointed and frustrated by the lack of attention and appreciation his books received. Nevertheless, *The Friends of Eddie Coyle* is now considered by many to be one of the greatest crime novels ever written.

*(35)* According to the passage, George V. Higgins wrote *The Friends of Eddie Coyle*
**1** because he believed that the novel would become a bestseller and enable him to quit the law profession to write full time.
**2** after becoming frustrated about the lack of awareness among ordinary Americans regarding the extent of criminal activity in the United States.
**3** because he wanted to show readers how hard lawyers worked in order to protect the victims of crime.
**4** after being inspired by what he found during the investigations he carried out while he was a lawyer.

*(36)* In the second paragraph, what do we learn about *The Friends of Eddie Coyle*?
**1** Higgins wanted to produce a novel which proved that the traditional rules of crime fiction still held true in modern times.
**2** The novel is unusual because Higgins tells the story through interactions between the characters rather than by describing specific events in detail.
**3** Higgins relied heavily on dialogue throughout the novel because he lacked the confidence to write long passages of narration.
**4** Although the novel provides an authentic description of the criminal world, Higgins did not consider it to be a true crime novel.

*(37)* Which of the following statements would the author of the passage most likely agree with?
**1** Despite the possibility that Higgins could have attracted a wider readership by altering his writing style, he remained true to his creative vision.
**2** The first book Higgins produced was poorly written, but the quality of his work steadily increased in the years that followed.
**3** It is inevitable that writers of crime novels will never gain the same level of prestige and acclaim as writers of other genres.
**4** It is unrealistic for writers of crime novels to expect their work to appeal to readers decades after it was first published.

# Mummy Brown

Thousands of years ago, ancient Egyptians began practicing mummification—the process of drying out the bodies of the dead, treating them with various substances, and wrapping them to preserve them. It was believed this helped the dead person's spirit enter the afterlife. Beginning in the twelfth century, however, many ancient mummies met a strange fate, as a market arose in Europe for medicines made using parts of mummies. People assumed the mummies' black color was because they had been treated with bitumen—a black, petroleum-based substance that occurs naturally in the Middle East and was used by ancient societies to treat illnesses. However, while ancient Egyptians did sometimes preserve mummies by coating them with bitumen, this method had not been used on many of the mummies that were taken to Europe. Furthermore, an incorrect translation of Arabic texts resulted in the mistaken belief that the bitumen used to treat mummies actually entered their bodies.

By the eighteenth century, advances in medical knowledge had led Europeans to stop using mummy-based medicines. Nevertheless, the European public's fascination with mummies reached new heights when French leader Napoleon Bonaparte led a military campaign in Egypt, which also included a major scientific expedition that resulted in significant archaeological discoveries and the documentation of ancient artifacts. Wealthy tourists even visited Egypt to obtain ancient artifacts for their private collections. In fact, the unwrapping and displaying of mummies at private parties became a popular activity. Mummies were also used in various other ways, such as being turned into crop fertilizer and fuel for railway engines.

One particularly unusual use of mummies was as a pigment for creating brown paint. Made using ground-up mummies, the pigment, which came to be known as mummy brown, was used as early as the sixteenth century, though demand for it grew around the time of Napoleon's Egyptian campaign. Its color was praised by some European artists, who used it in artworks that can be seen in museums today. Still, the pigment had more critics than fans. Many artists complained about its poor drying ability and other negative qualities.

Moreover, painting with a pigment made from deceased people increasingly came to be thought of as disrespectful—one well-known British painter who used mummy brown immediately buried his tube of the paint in the ground when he learned that real mummies had been used to produce it.

Even artists who had no objection to mummy brown could not always be certain its origin was genuine, as parts of dead animals were sometimes sold as mummy parts. Also, the fact that different manufacturers used different parts of mummies to produce the pigment meant there was little consistency among the various versions on the market. Additionally, the mummification process itself, including the substances used to preserve the bodies, underwent changes over time. These same factors make it almost impossible for researchers today to detect the presence of mummy brown in specific paintings. Given the pigment's controversial origins, however, perhaps art lovers would be shocked if they discovered that it was used in any of the paintings they admire.

(38) According to the author of the passage, why were ancient Egyptian mummies used to make medicines in Europe?
   **1** Disease was widespread in Europe at the time, so Europeans were willing to try anything to create effective medicines.
   **2** Because the mummies had not turned black in spite of their age, Europeans assumed they could provide health benefits.
   **3** Europeans mistakenly believed that a substance which was thought to have medical benefits was present in all mummies.
   **4** The fact that the mummies had religious significance to ancient Egyptians caused Europeans to believe they had special powers.

*(39)* What is one thing we learn about Napoleon Bonaparte's military campaign in Egypt?
**1** A number of leaders saw it as a reason to also invade Egypt, which led to the destruction of many ancient artifacts.
**2** It revealed information about ancient Egyptian culture that led Europeans to change their opinion of medicines made from mummies.
**3** It was opposed by wealthy Europeans, who thought it would result in their collections of ancient artifacts being destroyed.
**4** It led to an increased interest in mummies and inspired Europeans to use them for a number of purposes.

*(40)* The author of the passage mentions the British painter in order to
**1** provide an example of how the use of mummy brown was opposed by some people because it showed a lack of respect for the dead.
**2** explain why mummy brown remained popular among well-known artists in spite of its poor technical performance.
**3** give support for the theory that mummy brown was superior to other paint pigments because of its unique ingredients.
**4** describe one reason why some artists developed a positive view of mummy brown after initially refusing to use it.

*(41)* What is one thing that makes it difficult to determine whether a painting contains mummy brown?
**1** The substances that were added to the pigment to improve its color destroyed any biological evidence that tests could have detected.
**2** The way that ancient Egyptians prepared mummies changed, so the contents of the pigment were not consistent.
**3** Artists mixed the pigment with other types of paint before applying it to paintings, so it would only be present in very small amounts.
**4** The art industry has tried to prevent researchers from conducting tests on paintings because of concerns that the results could affect their value.

**4**

- Write an essay on the given TOPIC.
- Use TWO of the POINTS below to support your answer.
- Structure: introduction, main body, and conclusion
- Suggested length: 120-150 words
- Write your essay in the space provided on Side B of your answer sheet. <u>Any writing outside the space will not be graded.</u>

## TOPIC

*Should people stop using goods that are made from animals?*

## POINTS

- *Animal rights*
- *Endangered species*
- *Product quality*
- *Tradition*

# ●一次試験 · **Listening Test**

**There are three parts to this listening test.**

| | | | |
|---|---|---|---|
| **Part 1** | **Dialogues:** | 1 question each | Multiple-choice |
| **Part 2** | **Passages:** | 2 questions each | Multiple-choice |
| **Part 3** | **Real-Life:** | 1 question each | Multiple-choice |

※ Listen carefully to the instructions.

## Part 1

**No. 1**

1  His recent test scores.
2  Having to drop the class.
3  Finding a job.
4  Staying awake in class.

**No. 2**

1  The man could lose his job.
2  The man forgot his mother's birthday.
3  The man did not reply to her e-mail.
4  The man is not liked by the CEO.

**No. 3**

1  They take turns driving.
2  They were in a serious accident.
3  They work in a car repair shop.
4  Neither of them can drive next week.

**No. 4**

1  He cannot use his credit card.
2  He forgot to contact his card issuer.
3  He is short of cash today.
4  He lost his debit card.

**No. 5**

1  He is not suited to the call-center job.
2  He is learning the wrong interview techniques.
3  He should go to the interview he has been offered.
4  He should prioritize finding his dream job.

**No. 6**

1  Have the man take some tests.
2  Encourage the man to exercise more.
3  Give the man advice about work-related stress.
4  Recommend the man to a specialist.

**No. 7**

1. He will take his vacation later in the year.
2. He will meet with the personnel manager.
3. He will do what his manager asks him to do.
4. He will ask the woman to help him.

**No. 8**

1. It needs brighter colors.
2. It fits the company's image.
3. It is too similar to the current one.
4. It needs to be redesigned.

**No. 9**

1. He has not read Alice's book yet.
2. He cannot attend Alice's party.
3. He is no longer friends with Alice.
4. He was disappointed with Alice's book.

**No. 10**

1. Make sure she catches an earlier train.
2. Use a different train line.
3. Ride her bicycle to the office.
4. Go into the office on weekends.

**No. 11**

1. Garbage collection has become less frequent.
2. Garbage bags will become more expensive.
3. Local taxes are likely to rise soon.
4. The newspaper delivery schedule has changed.

**No. 12**

1. Try using some earplugs.
2. Have Ranjit talk to her neighbors.
3. Complain about her landlord.
4. Write a message to her neighbors.

## Part 2

*(A)*

**No. 13**
1 There are too many food choices available.
2 Schools often prepare uninteresting food.
3 They copy their parents' eating habits.
4 They have a desire to lose weight.

**No. 14**
1 Getting children to help make their own meals.
2 Encouraging children to play more sports.
3 Sometimes letting children eat unhealthy foods.
4 Rewarding children for eating vegetables.

*(B)*

**No. 15**
1 Ching Shih's pirates gained a number of ships.
2 Many pirate commanders were captured.
3 Most of the pirates were killed.
4 Ching Shih agreed to help the Chinese navy.

**No. 16**
1 She left China to escape punishment.
2 She gave away her wealth.
3 She formed a new pirate organization.
4 She agreed to stop her pirate operations.

*(C)*

**No. 17**
1 Their numbers increase at certain times.
2 They are being hunted by humans.
3 Their habitats have become smaller recently.
4 They have been eating fewer snowshoe hares.

**No. 18**
1 They only travel when looking for food.
2 They sometimes travel long distances.
3 They live much longer than other wildcats.
4 They always return to their original territories.

*(D)*

**No. 19**
1 Modern burial places are based on their design.
2 They were used for religious purposes.
3 They were only used by non-Christians.
4 The entrances were only found recently.

**No. 20**
1 Women used to be priests long ago.
2 The tunnels were not used as churches.
3 Few early Christians were women.
4 Priests used to create paintings.

*(E)*

**No. 21**
1 They often have successful family members.
2 They often have low levels of stress.
3 They may miss chances to enjoy simple pleasures.
4 They may make people around them happy.

**No. 22**
1 They do not need family support to stay happy.
2 Their incomes are not likely to be high.
3 Their positive moods make them more active.
4 They are more intelligent than unhappy people.

*(F)*

**No. 23**
1 They are becoming better at fighting disease.
2 Their numbers are lower than they once were.
3 Many of them are not harvested for food.
4 The waters they live in are becoming cleaner.

**No. 24**
1 Native American harvesting practices helped oysters grow.
2 Native American harvesting methods included dredging.
3 Native Americans still harvest oysters.
4 Native Americans only harvested young oysters.

## Part 3

*(G)*
**No. 25**

*Situation:* You are about to take a tour bus around a town in Italy. You want to join the guided walking tour. You hear the following announcement.

*Question:* Which bus stop should you get off at?

**1** Stop 4.
**2** Stop 7.
**3** Stop 9.
**4** Stop 13.

*(H)*
**No. 26**

*Situation:* You are abroad on a working-holiday program. You call the immigration office about renewing your visa and are told the following.

*Question:* What should you do first?

**1** Fill out an application online.
**2** Request salary statements from your employer.
**3** Show evidence of your savings.
**4** Obtain a medical examination certificate.

*(I)*
No. 27

***Situation:*** You are a supermarket manager. You want to reduce losses caused by theft. A security analyst tells you the following.

***Question:*** What should you do first?

**1** Give some staff members more training.
**2** Install more security cameras.
**3** Review customer receipts at the exit.
**4** Clearly mark prices for fruit.

*(J)*
No. 28

***Situation:*** You want a new washing machine. You currently own a Duplanne washing machine. You visit an electronics store in July and hear the following announcement.

***Question:*** What should you do to save the most money?

**1** Download the store's smartphone app.
**2** Apply for the cash-back deal.
**3** Exchange your washing machine this month.
**4** Buy a new Duplanne washing machine in August.

*(K)*
No. 29

***Situation:*** You see a suit you want in a local store, but it does not have one in your size. You do not want to travel out of town. A clerk tells you the following.

***Question:*** What should you do?

**1** Wait until the store gets some new stock.
**2** Have the clerk check the other store.
**3** Order the suit from the online store.
**4** Have the suit delivered to your home.

# ●二次試験・面接

※本書では出題例として2種類のカードを掲載していますが，本番では1枚のみ渡されます。
※面接委員の質問など，二次試験に関する音声はCDに収録されていません。

## 受験者用問題　カード　A

You have **one minute** to prepare.

This is a story about a couple that wanted to be involved with their community.
You have **two minutes** to narrate the story.

Your story should begin with the following sentence:
**One day, a husband and wife were going on a walk together.**

**No. 1**     Please look at the fourth picture. If you were the wife, what would you be thinking?

Now, Mr. / Ms. _____, please turn over the card and put it down.

**No. 2**     Do you think parents should participate in school events such as sports festivals?

**No. 3**     Do public libraries still play an important role in communities?

**No. 4**     Should more companies offer their employees flexible work schedules?

You have **one minute** to prepare.

This is a story about a woman who wanted to go on a trip.
You have **two minutes** to narrate the story.

Your story should begin with the following sentence:
**One day, a woman was talking with her friend.**

**No. 1**   Please look at the fourth picture.  If you were the woman, what would you be thinking?

Now, Mr. / Ms. _____, please turn over the card and put it down.

**No. 2**   Do you think it is good for university students to have part-time jobs?

**No. 3**   Do you think it is safe to give personal information to online businesses?

**No. 4**   Should the government do more to increase the employment rate in Japan?

CD作成協力●ELEC録音スタジオ　　本文デザイン●松倉浩・鈴木友佳

編集協力●一校舎　　　　　　　　　企画編集●成美堂出版編集部

**本書に関する正誤等の最新情報は，下記のアドレスで確認することができます。**
**https://www.seibidoshuppan.co.jp/support/**

上記URLに記載されていない箇所で正誤についてお気づきの場合は，書名・発行日・質問事項・ページ数・氏名・郵便番号・住所・FAX番号を明記の上，**郵送またはFAXで成美堂出版**までお問い合わせください。

**※電話でのお問い合わせはお受けできません。**

※本書の正誤に関するご質問以外にはお答えできません。また受験指導などは行っておりません。

※ご質問の到着確認後，10日前後に回答を普通郵便またはFAXで発送いたします。

　ご質問の受付期限は，2024年度の各試験日の10日前到着分までとさせていただきます。ご了承ください。

---

・本書の付属CDは，CDプレーヤーでの再生を保証する規格品です。

・CDプレーヤーで音声が正常に再生されるCDから，パソコンやiPodなどのデジタルオーディオプレーヤーに取り込む際にトラブルが生じた場合は，まず，そのソフトまたはプレーヤーの製作元にご相談ください。

・本書の付属CDには，タイトルなどの文字情報はいっさい含まれておりません。CDをパソコンに読み込んだ際，異なった年版や書籍の文字情報が表示されることがありますが，それは弊社の管理下にはないデータが取り込まれたためです。必ず音声をご確認ください。

---

このコンテンツは，公益財団法人 日本英語検定協会の承認や推奨，その他の検討を受けたものではありません。

## 英検®準1級過去6回問題集 '24年度版

2024年3月10日発行

編　者　成美堂出版編集部

発行者　深見公子

発行所　成美堂出版
　　　　〒162-8445　東京都新宿区新小川町1-7
　　　　電話(03)5206-8151　FAX(03)5206-8159

印　刷　株式会社フクイン

©SEIBIDO SHUPPAN 2024 PRINTED IN JAPAN
ISBN978-4-415-23808-1
落丁・乱丁などの不良本はお取り替えします
定価はカバーに表示してあります